W9-BRG-410

A FATAL FAMILY SECRET

BOOK ONE OF THE MORPHOSIS ME FILES

A NOVEL BY SAMANTHA MARKS

Hey Jada,
Hope you enjoy!
Dr. Sam

Copyrighted Material

Copyright © 2015 by Samantha Marks

Cover and art copyright @ 2016 by Jenny Zemanek of

Seedlings Design Studio

Divider artwork copyright © 2015 by Randy Alcalá

Book design and layout copyright © 2016 by Samantha Marks

This novel is a work of fiction. Names, characters, places and incidents are either products of the author's imagination or used fictitiously. Any resemblance to actual events, locales, or persons, living, dead, or undead, is entirely coincidental.

All rights reserved.

No part of this publication can be reproduced or transmitted in any form or by any means, electronic or mechanical, without permission in writing from Samantha Marks, www.samanthamarks.com

2nd Edition

ISBN 1943406014

Library of Congress number 8-124-778

First paperback edition: May 13, 2015

Printed in the United States of America

A Fatal Family Secret

Book One of The Morphosis.me Files

A Novel by Samantha Marks, Psy.D.

The Morphosis.me Files

A Fatal Family Secret (#1)

A Treacherous Social Game (#2)

A Perilous Blood Allegiance (#3) February 2017

A Noble Clan Legacy (#4) November 2017

DEDICATION

To my funny, smart, and beautiful daughter, Sophie. Thank you for putting up with Mommy the Writer.

ACKNOWLEDGEMENTS

Very special thanks to my husband, Rinaldo Alcalá. Without your love and support I never would have been able to realize my dream.

Thank you to my amazing writing coach, S.M. Boyce, who pushed me (sometimes dragged me) up the mountain to publication.

Thank you to my talented brother-in-law, Randy Alcalá, for the amazing artwork.

Thanks to all my beta readers, especially Tamara Orr. Your comments and encouragement were invaluable.

Thank you to my editors Kristi Holl and Chase Nottingham, my proofreader Allisyn Ma, and my formatter Jason Sharp.

A world of thanks to my parents, Andy and Jackie Marks. You were incredibly patient and tolerant of me and all my "crazy ideas," which allowed me to become the woman I am today.

TABLE OF CONTENTS

PROLOGUE: TWO YEARS AGO 1
CHAPTER ONE: THE FIRST DAY 5
CHAPTER TWO: THE BIRTHDAY 19
CHAPTER THREE: HALLOWEEN 33
CHAPTER FOUR: THE MORPH.........................48
CHAPTER FIVE: TRAUMA 64
CHAPTER SIX: THE DATE................................81
CHAPTER SEVEN: FRIENDS.............................99
CHAPTER EIGHT: ANNE 118
CHAPTER NINE: SECRETS..............................133
CHAPTER TEN: MIND.....................................147
CHAPTER ELEVEN: BODY 166
CHAPTER TWELVE: SOUL...............................188
CHAPTER THIRTEEN: BULLIES 204
CHAPTER FOURTEEN: FAMILY 222
CHAPTER FIFTEEN: FLY 238
EPILOGUE: KIDNAPPED 243

PROLOGUE
TWO YEARS AGO

"Mom, Dad, I'm home!" Kayleigh said, arriving from school. "My birthday's been awesome!"

It had been a great thirteenth birthday so far, Kayleigh thought, even with having to go to school. Her mom had woken her up with her favorite breakfast in bed—pancakes and waffles with bananas Foster and decaf coffee. Her dad had given her a gift card to buy some new songs, and already her Me3 page had over twenty congratulatory messages.

Kayleigh didn't even mind that she only spoke with five of the twenty people who had left messages on her Me3. Most of her class had befriended each other online but didn't ever speak in school. They would post messages, music, or photos on their pages and send stuff to each other but seldom actually hung-out.

Kayleigh dumped her leather backpack on the long wooden bench that ran along one side of the small mudroom. Water cascaded to the floor as she pulled off her purple rain hat, shook the water off, and let her wavy auburn hair tumble down her back. She hung her jacket on a small wooden peg above the bench, and she kicked off her boots. Her feet shoved into a pair of worn oxfords, she pushed open the door to the family room.

She paused midway, and her eyes widened. It looked like a tornado had gone through the house. The overturned couch partially blocked the door, its cushions strewn across the floor. Jagged cuts in the sofa's fabric revealed its stuffing. She squeezed through the doorway and climbed over the back of the couch. Glass crunched under her feet as she took a step into the room. Her mother's collection of delicate swan figurines lay in pieces on the floor, along with books, papers, and other knickknacks.

"Mom? Dad? What happened?"

A sharp pang of fear ripped through Kayleigh's chest. She could barely breathe. The blood drained from her face, her head began to spin, and her knees started to buckle. She swayed against the wall of the family room.

"No, don't. Deep breath." She willed herself to remain upright, and she slowly walked through the tossed family room and into the hallway. The family portraits that had lined the wall now lay broken on the floor.

She paused at the base of the steps and listened for sounds upstairs, unsure if she should continue farther into the house. A pile of debris spilled off the second floor landing and onto the stairs. She turned and looked at the front door, which stood open several inches. A light mist had blown in and dampened the hardwood of the foyer. She grabbed the phone on the hallway table. Her hands trembled.

Nine. One. One.

"I need help..."

No sound answered her, and Kayleigh realized the phone was dead. She fumbled in her pocket and remembered she had left her cell phone in her backpack in the mudroom. Her heart beat out of her chest, and her breath seemed to roar in her ears. The acid rose in her throat, and a wave of nausea crashed in her stomach. She slapped a hand over her mouth and stifled the urge to vomit.

"Ka...Katherine." A voice from across the house broke through her fear.

Only her father called her Katherine. Everyone else called her "Kayleigh," a nickname from her first and middle names: Katherine Leigh.

"Katherine." It was her father's voice. Raspy and weak, it came from his study on the far side of the first floor.

A surge of energy propelled her across the hallway and into the living room. Kicking aside debris, she pulled herself around the corner to the dining room and crashed through broken plates and torn linens. She raced through the back sunroom towards her father's study, dodging capsized flowerpots and upended armchairs.

Suddenly, her torso slammed into a hard object, which knocked her backwards onto the floor. She landed on her back, and the air whooshed out of her lungs. The left side of her chest throbbed with pain. A gurgle escaped her lips, and she couldn't get enough air. She grabbed the leg of an end table and pulled herself up to see what she had hit.

She blinked her eyes, trying to focus. She didn't see any large object blocking the way, but the light in front of the entrance to the study shimmered. A large patch of the room in front of the door was fuzzy compared to the space around it. The afternoon rays streamed in from a window and highlighted a small tree that sat next to the large blur. The edges around the leaves were hazy, and the entire plant and its pot seemed to be moving slowly out of the way. The branches cast no shadow but seemed to bounce the light off their surfaces. She looked back towards the dining room, and everything seemed flat and normal. When she looked again towards the study, the fern sat in the corner, still.

Kayleigh shook her head and wondered when her father had gotten that particular plant. The rest of the foliage in the sunroom was ferns, flowers, and other tropical varieties. She stood and wobbled on her feet before gaining her balance.

"Dad, Dad." She burst into the study. The state of the room matched the rest of the house. Books had been swiped off the shelves, papers littered the floor, and the antique armchairs had been ripped open. She saw her father's shoes sticking out from behind the heavy mahogany desk.

She ran to where he lay and knelt by his side.

"Katherine." He sighed with relief and struggled to sit up. His face was swollen, and his bronze skin was purple on one side. He held one arm protectively to his chest. He grimaced, and he drew in ragged breaths.

"Dad, what happened?" Kayleigh said.

"They took...they took..." he said and then coughed hard, wincing from what Kayleigh thought might be a broken arm.

"Dad, don't talk. I'll get help," she said, and started to rise.

"Wait," he grabbed her hand. "You don't understand. They took..." He coughed again, and red blood splattered across his chin.

"What? Who?" A cold shiver crossed the back of her neck, and she heard sirens in the background. A neighbor must have called the police.

Her dad struggled again to move, and his eyes filled with tears.

"Your mother."

CHAPTER ONE

THE FIRST DAY

TODAY

The breeze *was warm and smelled like grass and wildflowers. It lifted the hair off her forehead and pulled at the strands around her face. The long grass tickled her bare feet, and the sun warmed her face. She felt calm and safe. Instinctively, Kayleigh knew she was in Ireland, although she had never actually been there. She took a deep breath and smelled lavender. Her mother must be close by.*

A bird swept over her head and landed on a nearby weeping willow. The tree's graceful branches brushed the ground and created a dome-shaped hideaway. The sound of laughter resonated from inside.

"Mom, are you there?" Kayleigh asked. She ran to the tree, parting the branches with her hands. She stepped inside. "Mom, it's me!"

It was dark and cold underneath the green canopy. Kayleigh frowned. Something didn't feel right. She could no longer hear the buzzing of insects or the sound of the wind rustling the long grass. She peered into the darkness. "Mom?"

Suddenly the ground felt soft underneath her feet, and she started to sink. "Mom, help! Where are you?" She flailed her arms as the thick mud reached her knees. She grabbed a low-hanging limb to stop her descent but only succeeded in ripping off a handful of leaves. As the mud oozed up around her head, she tasted the moist earth filling her mouth. It tasted gritty and metallic. Her lungs starved for air.

The alarm went off.

Kayleigh bolted upright, eyes wide, heart racing. She took several ragged breaths and pulled at the neck of her nightgown. Her shoulders sagged as her bedroom bled into view. She glared at her alarm clock as it blared beside her.

6:30 a.m.

Kayleigh groaned and pulled the covers over her head.

"Ugh...the first day of school," she said, rolling onto her stomach. She pushed her fat tabby cat, Emilio, off the bed. He yawned, padded to the bay window seat, and curled up in a patch of sunlight.

The first day of school was not as exciting for Kayleigh as it was for some of her friends. She didn't look forward to seeing everyone after summer break and comparing beach stories. She didn't want to be reminded that they had grown older and were starting another school year. Besides, it seemed like everyone posted minute-to-minute updates on their Me3 pages, so she didn't need to be told how their summers had gone.

Kayleigh hated the passage of time because she desperately wanted to go back two years to when her mother was still at home and life didn't suck. She longed to return to when her mother would snuggle with her and tell her stories of Ireland, princes, princesses, and children who were turned into swans.

The New York police had investigated several leads but never found her mother. Neighbors had not been helpful; no one had seen anything. Her father said the attackers had hit him from the rear and knocked him behind the desk, so he didn't get a look at their faces. After a year, when the leads dried up, they declared the case closed. Detectives told her father there was nothing else they could do. He grieved by shutting himself away in his study, leaving Kayleigh stuck asking questions nobody could answer.

In the past two years, her classmates' theories on her mom's disappearance had gradually faded away. Starting high school was bound to stir up rumors again. The bullying, although not directly related to her mother's disappearance, came in waves and varied in intensity. Some days the mean girl would just throw a couple of mildly condescending comments her way, and some days she would call Kayleigh nasty names.

Kayleigh didn't like change, so she tried to pretend everything was the same. Sometimes when she could feel the panic rising in the back of her throat when she was crushed in a crowded hallway, she would stand against the lockers and practice "letting the world go fuzzy." At first the hallway lights were too bright, the students too loud, and her chest too tight. Her skin crawled, and her feet itched to run. If she stood sufficiently still for long enough, though, the lights would blur, the sounds would blend, and everything would become fuzzy.

It was then that her body became light, and her mind could drift off. She would see her mother's face again, smell her lavender perfume, and feel what it was like to be held close. Her mother, Órla, was beautiful in a way Kayleigh wished she might be some day. Her mother had had bright red hair, clear green eyes, and a smile that made Kayleigh feel safe and loved.

"Katherine, wake up." Her dad knocked.

Kayleigh groaned again.

"Katherine Leigh, you need to wake up," he said through her bedroom door. "It is the first day of school."

"I know. Just let me sleep through it," Kayleigh said and pulled the covers tighter over her head. The thick quilt blocked the sun that was coming up over the horizon and streaming into her room.

Her father knocked again. The door thudded against its frame, and the sound echoed in the drafty room. Her mother had talked about moving out of the old house as it was on the town's historic registry, but now there was no way her father would consider leaving. It was all they had left of her.

"Katherine, I am coming in."

Her father opened the door, which creaked on its hinges and scraped along the warped wooden floors. His slippers made a shuffling sound on the planks until he reached the small rug in front of the bed. He sat, and the bed sloped to one side under his weight.

"Katherine, *mi princesita*, you need to get up and get ready for school."

Kayleigh sighed and let him pull the quilt back, the quilt that her mother and grandmother had made with colorful scraps of fabric from Ireland. She squinted against the light and pushed her hair back from her face.

She stared at her father who was leaning over and looking at her from above his wire-rimmed reading glasses. He must have been enjoying the morning paper, she mused. "Professor Dad," as she often called him, was a history professor specializing in Hispanic studies at the local community college near Syracuse.

"It's time for school," he said softly.

"I know, Dad," she said. "Why don't I skip the first couple of days, just until the excitement dies down?"

"That would be too easy, *mi vida*. Come on. I'll make your favorite breakfast and drive you to school."

Her father went downstairs to make banana pancakes, and Kayleigh dragged herself into the shower and got ready for school. She pulled jeans and a T-shirt out of her closet and threw on a dark green sweater several sizes too large. She would probably be too hot since the cooler fall weather hadn't started yet, but she needed some armor. She pulled the cowl neck up to bury her nose in its soft yarn. It no longer smelled like her mother.

It was only a five minute car ride to Onondaga High School but out of walking distance. Her dad dropped her off at the front of the school just as the buses were leaving. Daiyu, her friend since preschool, was standing out front with Ben waiting for the first bell.

"Hey, why didn't you have to take the bus?" she asked. Daiyu, whose name meant "Black Jade" in Chinese, was always direct and to the point. "If we have to suffer on the bus, you should as well!" Thick black bangs framed her almond eyes that looked sternly at Kayleigh.

Kayleigh and Daiyu had been friends since they were both enrolled as three-year-olds at the Early Learning Center. Both intelligent and reserved, they quickly found each other among the wild kids climbing the book shelves and had been friends ever since. Ben, one of the kids bouncing off the walls, didn't become their friend until several years later.

"I wouldn't take the bus if I didn't have to," Ben said and punched Kayleigh on the shoulder. He reminded her of a puppy dog who hadn't grown into his feet: clumsy and playful.

The first bell rang in the distance. "Come on, guys. Let's go," Kayleigh said. "I'd rather not be late on the first day."

"Oh, relax," Ben said, but he opened the door.

A rush of cold air whooshed over Kayleigh, and she sighed. The administration had probably only turned on the air conditioner that morning. It smelled stale and musty inside.

"Here goes the first day of another long year," she muttered under her breath.

"Let the learning begin!" Daiyu said, her eyes gleaming.

Kayleigh always teased Daiyu about being a stereotypical Asian girl, but as far as Kayleigh could tell, Daiyu's parents, Mr. and Mrs. Sun, put no more pressure on her to be a perfect student than Daiyu Sun put on herself.

Kayleigh, on the other hand, was happy to be average. Not exactly honor roll, but still in honors classes, she accepted being in the middle somewhere...middle of the road GPA, middle of the alphabet, and middle of the class. She enjoyed being nondescript in both appearance and performance and happy to not call attention to herself.

"There you are. *Maidin mhaith!*" Bridget said, coming out of homeroom.

"*Ma-jin wah* what?" Ben said, looking up at Bridget, who was easily a foot taller than him.

"That's good morning in Irish Gaelic, Ben. I'd think you'd recognize it by now after two years of hearing it," she said, shaking her head. "I've practically got my host family speaking it after just a couple of years."

Bridget had moved to the States two years ago from Ireland, at the beginning of 7th grade, as part of a cultural exchange program. A large number of immigrants and people of Irish-ancestry lived in Massachusetts and across upstate New York. Bridget joked she would teach them all to speak Irish Gaelic again.

"Blame it on summer. I forget everything in summer, including how tall you are." Ben stretched up on his tiptoes but still only managed to reach her chin. Bridget grinned and looked down her porcelain nose at him.

"Silly man child," she said, using her thickest Irish accent and flipping her thick black curls off her shoulder, "when will ye learn that women are superior to ye wee men in every way?"

Certainly Bridget was superior to most girls, Kayleigh thought, since Bridget was tall, beautiful, and seemingly flawless. She already had curves, perfect ivory skin, and big blue eyes with thick dark lashes. Her long black hair never seemed to be out of place, and even at fifteen years old, she looked more like she belonged on a runway than in a classroom. It would be horribly annoying if she weren't so nice.

The four of them laughed, and Kayleigh felt a wave of relief wash over her. This felt normal, the four of them joking and teasing each other. She could almost forget that school was about to begin.

After checking in with their homeroom teachers, they arrived in Mr. Rhodes' room for health class. Kayleigh was glad they were starting out the year with their health unit, which was preferable to being pummeled by dodgeballs or losing a lung on the track field.

"Sit down, everyone!" Mr. Rhodes said as the second bell rang out. "Welcome to Onondaga High School. Let's call roll before we begin the first period. Nathan Arscott."

"Here." A low voice from the back of the class answered, which was not the squeaky voice Kayleigh had expected. Surprised, she turned in her seat to look at Nate. He was no longer a chubby blond Boy Scout. He had grown half a foot, lost maybe twenty pounds, and updated his personal style with a striped tee and a blazer.

"Whoa, when did he get hot?" Bridget whispered to Kayleigh. "I thought boys were usually late bloomers."

Kayleigh blushed and shushed Bridget.

"Bridget Byrne," Mr. Rhodes called.

"Present," Bridget answered. She gave the teacher a Cheshire smile.

As the teacher called roll, Kayleigh thought about the fact that she hadn't fully bloomed yet, although Nathan apparently had. She still felt like she was trapped in the body of a fourteen-year-old child. Her father may have awkwardly taken her to buy bras last year, but that did not mean she could fill them.

"Katherine Paz-Purcell." The teacher jolted Kayleigh from her musings.

"Yes?" Kayleigh said and heard someone snicker in the back of the room. "I mean, here." She felt her cheeks grow hot, and she sank in her chair.

"Daydreaming on the first day?" Mr. Rhodes said, giving her a disapproving look. "Daiyu Sun," he continued with the roll call.

"Here, Mr. Rhodes," Daiyu said. She looked at Kayleigh and frowned.

After a few more names, Mr. Rhodes came to the bottom of the list. "Benjamin Wolfson."

Ben raised his hand in mock salute. "Yes, sir, Mr. Rhodes. Ready and eager to learn, sir." A few students laughed, but Kayleigh rolled her eyes. She wished Ben didn't try so hard to be the class clown. Last year, Ben had tried to get everyone to start calling him "Wolf," in an attempt to be cooler, probably, but the nickname didn't stick.

Mr. Rhodes did not smile. He said, "Lovely, Ben, I'm glad you came back with such a positive attitude. You can start today's conversation, therefore, on the male reproductive system."

Ben turned beet red and stammered "Uh, I have one?"

The class erupted into laugher, but Ben nodded and waved them on.

"Yes, Mr. Wolfson." Mr. Rhodes said. "Begin reading on page seventy-two."

As Ben listed off the parts of the male reproductive system, Kayleigh cringed and suddenly doubted the idea that Health was better than P.E. dodgeball.

"Thank you, Ben, for the overview of the male reproductive system," Mr. Rhodes said. "May I have a volunteer to read the overview of the female reproductive system?"

"How about Kayleigh?" A haughty voice spoke from the front of the class. Emma Vanderweele turned around in her chair and stared at Kayleigh with a nasty look in her icy blue eyes.

Kayleigh froze, and her breath caught in her throat. Emma, the original mean girl, had started bullying her in kindergarten when she led the entire class to chant "Kayleigh Pee-Pee." As they got older the taunts changed from simple name calling to vile insults. The bullying occurred daily all through elementary school, until Bridget arrived on the first day of seventh grade. She'd told Emma "to stuff it" and shoved her on the playground.

"Stay in yer own lane, Emma." Bridget spoke up immediately. She leaned forward and stared at the blonde, silently daring her to open her mouth again.

Emma glared at Bridget and looked as if she might say something, but then turned around in her chair back towards the teacher. He merely stood there glancing back and forth among the three girls, not sure what to do. Eventually, he started reading where Ben had left off, and the class gradually turned its attention back to the book.

The rest of the morning went by fairly quickly. Kayleigh concentrated on collecting the syllabi for her classes, organizing her agenda, and staying out of Emma's way. Emma always acted as if she were better than everyone, and although Kayleigh had to admit she was pretty and had nice clothes, her attitude made her ugly. Although, she still managed to have her "mean girl posse," two wannabes who followed her around and hearted all her posts on Me3.

Kayleigh entered the lunchroom and saw Bridget, Daiyu, and Ben sitting with mutual friends. Kayleigh looked around quickly for Emma as she sat down, hoping Emma had been scheduled for another lunch period.

"Hi, everyone. *Buen provecho,*" she said out of habit, meaning "bon appetite." Her father had drilled into her several Puerto Rican customs, such as wishing everyone a good meal when you see them eating or about to eat. It was quite annoying, actually, when she would visit her Abuelita during the summers and at least twenty people would comment while she was eating. Each person walking by who said *buen provecho* would require a *gracias* in return, or at least a nod if Kayleigh's mouth was full of food. She thought it unpleasant to eat in public.

"Hey girl, what's up?" Martin said as he helped her onto the bench.

"Nothing much, Martin, just trying to survive the first day," Kayleigh said. She and Martin had been friends since middle school when they'd been paired for a science project.

"Yeah, I heard you already had a run-in with the queen bee," he said.

"Don't you dare dethrone me, Martin," Bridget said and leaned over to grab his hand. "How can you be king if your queen doesn't like you!"

"Milady." Martin laughed, bowed his head and gave her hand a kiss. "I heard you defended our girl against the witch."

"Yes, she did. Thank you, Bridget," Kayleigh said. "I didn't expect her to attack on the first day of school. Although this was pretty mild compared to when she wrote fugly on my locker last year."

"Or when she hid your clothes after gym class, and you had to spend the rest of the day in your uniform," Daiyu added. Kayleigh squinted her eyes and wrinkled her nose at her friends.

"The best defense is a good offense, Coach always says." Martin Williams was tall and muscled and had already made the varsity football team. He was thinking about trying to go pro, although his father wanted him to study history and law.

"Yeah, Kayleigh, 'Be Prepared,'" Ben said and held up three fingers like a Boy Scout.

"Okay, guys," Daiyu said. "You'll kill Kayleigh with clichés before she even gets a chance to take on Emma."

"How about anonymously trolling her Me3 page?" Natalie said. She was a self-declared "hacktivist" and regularly monitored all social media sites and webpages. "It's as offensive, I mean, on the offensive, as it gets."

"People," Daiyu said, "the last thing Kayleigh should do is get sucked into a cat fight with a Vanderweele."

"How about something more traditional, then? Say swords at dawn?" Bridget said, making a swishing motion with her arm.

"I vote for mud wrestling!" Ben said and gave Martin a high five.

"Thank you all for your suggestions," Kayleigh said, "but I think I'll stick to freezing like a deer in headlights or running away in a cold sweat." She sighed and finished her peanut butter and jelly sandwich.

"Come on, Kay, toughen up," Bridget said. "She's just a bloody bucket of snots!"

"Thanks, Bridget, and ew."

"You know what I mean. If you show the haters like her that they bother you, then it gives them just what they want—

to feel powerful. She only picks on you to avoid feeling insecure and small."

"Great, so whom should I pick on, then?"

There was a momentary silence around the table.

"I'm sorry, guys, I don't mean to be a Debbie Downer." Kayleigh heard the bell ring and got up to throw her trash away. "I will try to have more of a sense of humor tomorrow, I promise. There might even be mud."

The rest of the day went by in a blur, and before Kayleigh could think more about Emma and catfights, she was getting off the bus in front of her house. Mrs. O'Neill, their next-door neighbor, was in her front yard raking leaves. Kayleigh watched her gather them into large piles and then scoop them into trash bags. It was hard to believe she was eighty-one years old.

"Hi, Mrs. O'Neill," Kayleigh said.

"Hi, dearie. How was your first day of school?"

"It was as expected, I guess."

"Listen, the postman came by, but since your father wasn't home, he left the little package with me." She pulled a small rectangular package from the pocket of her flowered housedress and handed it to Kayleigh. It was wrapped in brown paper and twine and had no return address.

"Oh, okay, thanks," Kayleigh said, "I didn't think they did that." Puzzled, she looked at Mrs. O'Neill's wrinkled face and innocent smile. Then she shrugged her shoulders and went inside.

She dumped her books on the mudroom bench, hung up her jacket, and took out her phone. She wandered into the kitchen and poured herself some juice. Her father wouldn't be home until much later, but the crockpot on the counter was emitting an aroma of beef and potatoes. Her father wasn't much of a cook, but he could chop up ingredients and throw them into the pot before he left for the college every day.

Kayleigh grabbed a bag of pretzels and sat at the large kitchen table. It was a rectangular, wooden table with two long benches, all of it stained a dark walnut. Her mother had said that when she was little, her father built it so that all seven children and three adults (two parents and "Nanna") could sit around the same table. As an only child, Kayleigh couldn't imagine having that many siblings and that much chaos. Her father also came from a large family, so she often wondered why they had stopped at just her.

A quick check of her Me3 page didn't show any comments of interest, so she put her phone on the table and looked at the package. Her name and address was on the front, but there was no return address. It didn't look like the post office had stamped it, either, but she couldn't think of a reason Mrs. O'Neill would lie about the mailman dropping it off.

Mrs. O'Neill had moved in shortly after her mother disappeared, and she brought them soup, casseroles, and cookies all throughout those chaotic first weeks. She often brought over fresh flowers from her garden and would sit and drink tea with her father. Kayleigh considered her a grandmother.

She pulled the string, and the back paper unfolded to reveal a small jewelry box and a crinkled note. Her hands shook a little as she unfolded the beige parchment.

Your mother thinks you should have this.

Kayleigh gasped and dropped the paper on the table as if it had scalded her fingers. She held her breath and ripped the top off of the box.

Inside, nestled in green felt, was a silver necklace. Kayleigh took it out and held it up. The chain was made of many intricately entwined loops that glinted in the late afternoon sunlight. On the strand hung an old antique key that someone had made into a pendant. At the top of the key was an engraving of a swan, wings spread and long neck stretched about to fly. The necklace felt heavy in her hands.

Your mother thinks you should have this.

A wave of sadness washed over Kayleigh, and she blinked back tears. How was it possible someone had sent this to her so many years after her mother's disappearance?

Beep beep!

Kayleigh jumped at the sound of her cell phone. That sound signaled she had received a message routed through one of the social media sites. She wiped the tears from her eyes with the back of her sweater, her mother's sweater, and picked up the phone.

Anonymous: Poor baby. No mother's shoulder to cry on.

CHAPTER TWO

THE BIRTHDAY

It had been over a month since the necklace arrived. She'd hesitated to show it to her father until she knew what it meant and who had sent it, but Mrs. O'Neill never seemed to be home when she went to ask for more details. Googling the design of the necklace only led to pages of swan jewelry on the Internet, but nothing was an exact match.

Kayleigh again held the note in her hand, as she had every day since it had arrived on the first day of school. She rubbed her thumb lightly over the four large creases in the paper and traced the smaller wrinkles of the parchment.

Your mother thinks you should have this.

Kayleigh felt a flash of pain every time she read those words. She woke up early every morning and stared at it in bed, wondering about who'd sent her the necklace and why. It was consuming so much brainpower that her grades were more dismal thus far than average. Plus, she'd spent too much time scanning her mother's missing persons page to see if anyone had posted new information. Her father would be surprised when the first quarter interim reports arrived this week and showed C and D grades.

Her father knocked on her door. "*Buenos días*, Katherine, time to get up."

"I'm awake, Dad," Kayleigh said.

"Excellent. Happy birthday!" He opened the door a crack. "*Feliz cumpleaños.*"

"Ugh, just let me skip my birthday." She rolled over and tucked the note back under her pillow.

"Not a chance...*Levántate*. Get up!" He tried to sound firm, but he hesitated in the doorway. She knew he was wondering how much space to give her. Her mother had always taken the parenting lead, and now that Kayleigh was an adolescent, both she and her father felt her mother's absence.

"I'm up...I'm up...jeez." She sat up and rolled her eyes at him.

Kayleigh didn't want to give her father a hard time. He was doing the best he could as a single parent. He was just very different from her mom. She had been bold and always laughing, while he was quiet and serious. Her mom was a nurse who had cared for everyone while talking their ears off with her stories about growing up in Ireland. Her dad, on the other hand, grew up in Puerto Rico and had amazing stories, but he shared them infrequently.

"*Feliz cumpleaños, mi princesita.*" Her father sat on the bed and smiled at her. He handed her a flat present wrapped in brown paper.

"Dad, I'm pretty sure that turning fifteen means you can't call me your 'little princess' anymore." She looked down at the package and recognized the plain brown paper, which matched her previous gift. Of course that packaging paper had to be in every post office and mail shop all over the world.

She unwrapped the present to find a framed ink drawing on thick parchment paper. It showed a young girl sitting underneath a large tree. The girl was leaning against the trunk with her eyes closed, a peaceful expression on her face. The fine lines of the artist showed great detail, such as the leaves, the bark, the girl's dress, and the girl's long hair. The drawing had a hint of color, as if the colors were once brilliant but had faded over time.

"Dad, it's beautiful." Kayleigh turned to him and looked into his soft brown eyes. "Thank you."

Her father sniffed. "You will always be my little princess, you know, no matter how old you get. Exactly as your mother was always my 'Queen of Everything.'" He reached out to grab a messy strand of her hair. "You look so much like her."

"Thank—wait, what?" She looked at him intently. "*Was*, Dad? When did you start using the past tense?" She pushed past him and got out of bed. "We don't know what happened. There is no evidence that she died, so she still *is* and will always be your 'Queen of Everything.'" She ran her hands through her hair and paced in front of the bed. "Although I must say that is a stupid title, and I had no idea you were so sappy."

His face fell and suddenly he looked older and fragile. She noticed the lines etched into his forehead, around his eyes, and at the corners of his mouth. *Lineas de expresión*, her Abuelita always called them, but to Kayleigh they looked less like lines of expression and more like lines of pain.

Seeing his hurt took the wind out of her rant, and she plopped back down on the bed next to him. She leaned into his shoulder and took his leathery hand. "I'm sorry. That was really mean. I shouldn't have said that. I miss her, too."

Her father was quiet for a moment. When he finally spoke, his voice was steady. "Honestly, Kayleigh, I do not know if she is dead or not. The police had very few clues, and I was not much help. I didn't think your mom had any enemies. After two years and no new clues, I have chosen to believe she is gone, and I am trying to move on. Remaining in limbo is not healthy for anyone." He let go of her hand, patted her leg and got up. "I'll go make your breakfast."

She watched her dad walk to the door. He paused before leaving and turned to her. "In my culture, a girl's fifteenth birthday is a time to celebrate her becoming a woman. We hold a *Quinceañera*, or a party, with family and friends to dance, eat food, and tell stories. It is a rite of passage."

"Well, I'm not one for parties, Dad."

"I know." He left and closed the door.

Kayleigh went to her jewelry box, a dark wooden box with Celtic knots carved around the edges. She took a small green silk pouch from the box and pulled out the delicate silver chain. At the end hung the silver key, old and ornate, with the swan curled on the top.

"What does this mean?" she asked herself.

She slipped the necklace on. Immediately, a strange shiver shot through her body. Her skin felt light and flushed, like a sunburn. In the mirror, her face looked golden and seemed to glow. Her hair was bright and copper-colored, and her eyes a clear green. The necklace glinted and sparkled, and her entire body shimmered for a second. Then it abruptly stopped.

She blinked and looked at herself again. "What was that?" She looked dull again, her hair a muddy red, her eyes more brown than green, and the necklace looked flat and tarnished against her freckled skin. "Great, I turn fifteen, and I start hallucinating."

She returned the necklace to the jewelry box and finished getting ready for school. Downstairs, she grabbed a pancake to go and kissed her father goodbye. For the beginning of October, it was unseasonably cold, so she grabbed her winter jacket and knitted hat. Ben and Daiyu were already at the bus stop.

"Happy birthday!" Daiyu said.

"Congrats," Ben said. "You've survived another year as a teenager!"

"It's not that bad, Ben," Kayleigh said.

"Yes, it is, the land of teen angst," Ben added. "Where you have to worry about zits, body hair, and random boners. Well, maybe you don't have to worry about that last one." He shrugged and looked embarrassed.

Kayleigh knew about Ben's two-year crush on her. He had asked her to dance at his Bar Mitzvah, and it was sweaty and awkward. When she'd felt one of the random you-know-whats against her leg, she freaked out and left the dance floor. They both pretended it had never happened.

"Ben, don't be so negative," Daiyu said. "There are plenty of wonderful things to look forward to as a teenager."

"Yeah, like what?" he countered.

"Well, there's driving."

"In a year, not now. Tell me something that we can do now."

"How about PG-13 movies?" she said. "We can go to the movies without our parents."

"Oh, exciting. The movies," he said, waving jazz hands at her. "Are we old enough to hold hands in the dark, too, or make out in the balcony?"

"Ben, stop it!" Daiyu blushed and pushed him. It wasn't a secret that she had harbored a crush on Ben much longer than Ben had crushed on Kayleigh.

The bus arrived, and a voice shouted from the window, "*Oi*, chop chop, we haven't got all day!"

"Love you, too, Bridget!" Ben answered, and they boarded.

Bridget had saved them several seats in the middle of the bus. Kayleigh pushed her way down the aisle and tried not to bump everyone with her backpack.

Emma was sitting on the edge of her seat with her knees blocking the way. "Good morning, *Señorita*. I hear birthday wishes are in order?" she said with a smirk.

"Yes, Emma. Excuse me." Kayleigh tried to ignore her and push past.

"Hey, kids, sit down or fall over," the bus driver yelled back to them. "I'm on a schedule." He resumed driving.

Emma rolled her eyes at the driver and didn't move her legs. The bus bumped along the old residential road, and Kayleigh grabbed the seats to keep her balance.

"Leave her alone, Emma," Bridget said from behind her.

"I was just trying to respect Kayleigh's culture," Emma said. "That's why she has two last names, right?" She waved one hand at Bridget and turned back to Kayleigh. "That must get rather cumbersome, doesn't it, Kayleigh? One last name would be easier, wouldn't it?"

"Purcell was my mother's last name," Kayleigh said quietly.

"Oh, that's right," Emma continued, looking at her mean girl posse of Hannah and Madison for support and gradually talking louder so the rest of the bus could hear. "Your mother was Irish, and your father's the Hispanic. I forget you're one of those mixed-races that are popping up everywhere." She pulled her long blonde hair out of her scarf and adjusted her headband.

Kayleigh went still in the middle of the aisle. The bus had gone quiet except for the rumble of the motor. She could hear her heart beating in her ears and feel the muscles in her legs tighten. Her hands went cold and her nose began to tingle. *Don't panic, Kayleigh. Get yourself together. She's just a girl.* Kayleigh shook her head to clear her thoughts and felt a shimmer move up her body. It was the same strange sensation she had felt this morning when she put the necklace on.

"Bugger off, Emma," Bridget said, appearing at Kayleigh's side. "You forget that you 'Amuricans' are all mixed compared to the rest of the world. Even the Vander*whats*!"

Emma's eyes widened, and she started to stand. Bridget put one hand on her shoulder and swiftly shoved her back down in her seat as she kicked Emma's legs out of the aisle. She grabbed Kayleigh's wrist and pulled her past the other girls.

"In a million years we'll all have brown skin, with all the races mixing together," Bridget muttered as they took their seats, "yet a beastly such as Emma will still think she's better."

"Bridget, be careful," Daiyu, the voice of reason, said. "I get that Emma's a pain and a bully, but you'll be the one in trouble if you put your hands on her."

"Well, I'd do less if our deer here did more." Bridget looked over at Kayleigh, who felt like jumping out the window. "Why do you let her talk to you like that?"

Kayleigh didn't have an answer, and they rode to school without further comments. When they arrived, Bridget got up quickly and pushed past the other students to leave first. Kayleigh saw the anger in her movements but didn't understand why her best friend felt the need to defend her so strongly. Friends protected each other, but Bridget seemed to take the bullying more personally than she did.

Emma glanced back at her briefly, then tilted her head and tossed her hair. They really were rather alike, Emma and Bridget, although only one used her power for good.

The morning seemed to drag on as Kayleigh thought about what Bridget had said. Why didn't Kayleigh fight back? Her best friend might be too aggressive and would get herself into trouble, but there must be something Kayleigh could do besides freak out and say nothing.

The lunchroom was crowded today, and Kayleigh found Ben and Daiyu sitting at the end of a long table with Martin and Natalie.

"Hey, guys," she said. "No sign of Bridget yet?"

"Give her a chance to cool down," Daiyu said. "She'll be around."

"Kayleigh should be the one upset, from what I hear," Martin said. "Emma's a real 'Mean Girl,' and for some reason, she's got it in for Kayleigh this year."

"Uh, Kayleigh, did you see what she posted on her Me3 page about an hour ago?" Natalie asked, her eyes solemn. She held out the computer, but she seemed to hesitate.

Kayleigh took the laptop from Natalie and scanned the page. There was a big selfie of Emma in the corner of the page, looking like a beauty queen. Her tagline read, "You have to learn the rules of the game. And then you have to play better than anyone else."

Scrolling down, she skipped past the symbol for Sounds, which would take you to the user's music posts, and she rolled her eyes at the Images icon, which indicated there were 2,287 pictures and photos. She clicked on the icon for Words, which opened her string of peeps. Peeps, announced by a fancy "P," were short comments about people, and in Emma's case, usually nasty. She had posted one every class period.

P: Had a run-in on the bus with some weak sauces

P: Fugly Kayleigh you need to go away

P: Poser get back on the boat and go home

"What do you want to do, Kayleigh?" Natalie asked.

"Nothing. Just ignore her." She tried to look calm, but inside, she wanted to run off and hide until graduation. The word fugly especially stung, and she self-consciously tugged at her shirt. She looked around the lunchroom for any sign of Bridget.

"Ignore her?" Ben said. "I can't ignore being called lame."

"And she was racist," Daiyu said. "We should tell the administration."

"No, really. I don't want to start an all-out war with her," Kayleigh said.

"Girl, you may not want a war," Martin said, "but them's fightin' words. I can check with my dad about slander, libel, defamation, or whatever you call it." His father was a civil rights attorney who had named him after Martin Luther King.

"Thanks, Counselor," Kayleigh said, "but I doubt criminal charges would stick. I'd rather do nothing."

"Well, you may not want to do anything," Natalie said, "but I'm feeling like crashing her account." Natalie took back the laptop and typed away.

"No, Nat, don't," Kayleigh said. "You're as bad as Bridget. Emma may be a bully, but I'm sure hacking is illegal."

"I'm not a hacker. I'm a hacktivist, and this is a public service." She kept clacking on the keyboard. "Emma needs to learn she can't treat people like they're garbage."

"So then how about Daiyu's idea? I can go to Mr. Constantine."

"Too late!" She smacked the return key and spun the computer around. The screen fluttered for a moment, went dark, and then the words "404 Not Found" popped up against a stark white screen. "Her page is no more."

"WHAT!" They heard a shriek from across the cafeteria. Emma stood and tapped furiously at her tablet.

"What happened to my Me3?" she said, and grabbed Hannah's phone. "Where is my page?" Hannah cringed and inched away from Emma. Madison swiped at her phone and looked confused.

"My work here is done," Natalie said with a smile and packed up her laptop.

At that moment, a series of chirps filled the cafeteria, and people took out their phones. Kayleigh felt the phone in her pocket vibrate and then chirp. She retrieved it and clicked on the Nony app. It allowed users in a small radius to share anonymous messages.

Anonymous: Look at Kayleigh.

Kayleigh froze and immediately felt eyes on her. She slowly picked up her head and saw people either looking for her or already staring. She realized that she had stopped breathing.

Chirp chirp. Nony apps chirped all over the room.

Anonymous: Keep watching. Wait for it.

Kayleigh turned red and still hadn't taken a breath. She stood and almost tripped over the bench.

"Hey, baby girl, shake it off," Martin grabbed her hand.

Natalie connected her phone to the laptop and frantically typed. "I can't figure out who it's coming from."

"Come on, Kayleigh. They're just baiting you," Ben said. "Don't pay any attention."

Kayleigh couldn't ignore the attention of the room trained at her. She felt their eyes draining her of energy, and her legs wouldn't work. A blur of people swam in front of her eyes as the room spun, and the lights dimmed. The roar of her pulse in her ears drowned out the confused whispers, comments, and sniggers. Her phone vibrated again, and she glanced down at the one word message. Her limbs grew weaker as the room went dark. She crumpled on the floor.

Anonymous: Timber.

Kayleigh woke up in the nurse's office, lying on a cot with a cold washcloth on her forehead. The back of her head throbbed, and she felt sick to her stomach. Across the room, Mrs. Rouhani, the nurse, and Mr. Stanley, the school psychologist, whispered and gestured toward Kayleigh.

"What happened?" she asked, and tried to rise to a sitting position.

"Kayleigh, *Joon*, dear, do not yet sit up," Mrs. Rouhani said, addressing her with the Farsi word for "dear-one." She took the washcloth off Kayleigh's forehead and smoothed her hair. "Rest, please. You bumped your head when you fainted. Your father is on his way to take you home."

Kayleigh felt soothed looking into Mrs. Rouhani's large dark eyes and listening to her even voice. Her long dark hair was pulled into a braid that hung over one shoulder and to her waist. "Mr. Stanley is here to talk to you while you wait."

"Hi, Kayleigh." Mr. Stanley smiled and sat in a chair next to the cot. "How's your head?"

"It hurts," Kayleigh said.

"Can you tell me how you felt immediately before you fainted?"

"I couldn't breathe. The room began to spin."

"How about an emotional type of feeling? What do you remember?"

"Uh..." Kayleigh paused, not sure what to say. Emotions were uncomfortable things to share with total strangers.

"I'll bet you're thinking you don't know me very well, so why should you tell me how you felt?" Mr. Stanley smiled and leaned back in the chair. "I get that a lot, despite the fact you teenagers are notorious for sharing more on social media than you do in person."

Kayleigh blushed and looked away, remembering the Nony messages.

"I can imagine getting anonymous messages in a crowded cafeteria would be disconcerting," he said.

"I was confused," Kayleigh said. Without hurry, she sat up straight and saw a glass of water on the side table. She took a slow drink and thought again about being in the cafeteria. "The lights were bright, everyone was staring at me, and I didn't know why. The message implied something was going to happen to me."

"Have you ever fainted before?" he asked.

"I don't think so, but I sometimes feel light-headed, and I can't breathe."

Her father arrived and started towards her, only to pause when he saw the counselor talking to Kayleigh. He instead spoke to Mrs. Rouhani in hushed tones.

Mr. Stanley continued his questioning. "Your friends reported that you were breathing heavily, actually, and sweating. It seems like you might have had a panic attack. Do you remember the first time this happened?"

"When my mom..." She stopped and looked at him. He was older and seemed wise, with kind gray-blue eyes. That didn't mean he could be trusted, though.

"I understand. That was a difficult time for you and your father. You didn't feel safe."

"It was awful." Kayleigh sighed. "No one could tell us who took her." She gestured to her father, who stood close to Mrs. Rouhani, her hand on his arm. "Someone attacked him and took my mother. He couldn't defend her." Anger began to simmer under her skin, and she felt warm. This was a different feeling from the cold clammy grip of panic. She suddenly became aware of every pore on her skin, all five million of them. Like this morning, she felt sunburned or flushed. Looking down at her hand, her fingers seemed to shimmer. She took a deep breath, and the shimmer stopped.

"A bunch of messages on Nony shouldn't be as scary as my mother disappearing, but I fainted. I don't understand."

"Bullies can be pretty scary, though," Mr. Stanley said. "Especially when they hide behind social media to intimidate. That can feel threatening. Have you had an argument with anyone recently?"

Kayleigh wanted to tell him about Emma and her mean comments, both on the bus and on Me3. The problem was that it would expose two of her friends, since Bridget had shoved Emma, and Natalie had crashed her profile page. Kayleigh knew that what Emma was doing was wrong, but she wasn't sure that Bridget and Natalie were so right. Telling the school psychologist about Emma might lead to her friends getting in trouble. She didn't want that.

"No, not really. Normal teenager stuff." Kayleigh tried to sound flippant.

"Normal teenager stuff should not include bullying, Kayleigh. Adolescence is hard enough without you guys turning on each other."

"In theory," Kayleigh said.

"Well, I'll leave you to mull that over. Let me go and have a word with your father."

Kayleigh looked down at her hand and realized it had formed a fist. Another bolt of energy swirled through her and blurred the freckles on her skin. For a moment her skin appeared brown and translucent.

Kayleigh took a deep breath and counted to ten in an effort to regain control of herself. Mr. Stanley had a hand on her father's shoulder and was whispering something to him, but Kayleigh could only make out the word "attack." Her father flinched. Great, Mr. Stanley was either telling him that she had been verbally attacked by another student through social media, or had experienced a panic attack. Possibly both.

Her father came to her with a concerned look and took her face in his hands. *"Como te sientes?"* He tilted Kayleigh's head back and forth, brushing the hair from her face as if looking for wounds.

"I feel fine, really," Kayleigh said, embarrassed. She lightly pushed his hands away. "I've got a hard head. I'm pretty sure the biggest wound is on the inside."

"Your pride will recover as well, with time," he said.

Kayleigh gathered her backpack and jacket and winced at the slight pain in the back of her head. "Let's go, please. Take me home."

"Cedro, thank you so much for coming," Mrs. Rouhani said. She placed her hand again on his arm.

Her father put his own hand over hers and gazed at the nurse. His face softened. "Soraya, thank you." With his Puerto Rican accent, the *r* rolled over his tongue like a ripple in a pond.

Kayleigh wondered when her father had met the nurse before. She couldn't recall any time they would have visited long enough to address each other by their first names, and yet they seemed awfully comfortable with each other.

As she was walking out the door, she heard Mr. Stanley call after her, "Oh, and happy birthday."

CHAPTER THREE
HALLOWEEN

"I vaaant to suuuck your bloooood!" the Dracula decoration waved its arms and sang at Kayleigh.

"No offense," she told it, "but you don't look much like a sexy Euro Vamp." She set it down on the entrance table inside the front door and grabbed the next scary attraction.

"Talking to yourself again?" Bridget said, walking in from the family room with a plastic ghost. "How about I hang this on the front door?"

"Yes, great," Kayleigh said, less than enthusiastic about the upcoming holiday. "So the entire neighborhood will know to stop here on Halloween."

"What's it matter to you, though? Your father is the one who has to answer the door. We'll be at the Spook Fest."

"Ugh, no. I already told you I don't want to go to the dance." Kayleigh sat at the bottom of the stairs. She watched Bridget hang the ghost and a Happy Halloween sign on the door. "Why is that dance so important to you?"

"When else during the entire year do you get to be someone or something else? You can dress in completely different clothes, different hair, different attitude." Bridget put one hand on her hips, swinging them back and forth in mock seduction. "You can be whomever you want!"

"Nah, it still feels like me in a costume," Kayleigh said, unconvinced. "Besides, how can I decide to be someone else for an evening when I can't even figure out who I am now?"

"What's there to figure out?" Bridget asked.

"I don't know. I just feel like I'm not myself lately, but I really can't tell you who I'm supposed to be. Everybody designs their Me3 profiles as if they know exactly where they fit in the hierarchy of high school. Am I a nerd, an emo, a goth, a prep, or a jock?"

Bridget snorted and raised one eyebrow at Kayleigh. "Do you really want me to answer that?"

"Ha, funny. No."

Kayleigh chose a mask from the pile of decorations. It was a skull, with flowers and vines in bright colors swirling around the eye and nose holes and across the forehead. Her father had purchased it on a trip to Mexico last year.

"I can't keep track of Me3 and worry about what my body is doing. Although you can tell what's happening just by looking at my face." She set the mask down and scratched lightly at some acne on the side of her cheek. "I'm so not thrilled about all the extra hair, and I could definitely do without PMS. The only good thing is I think I'm a couple of inches taller."

"And you've finally filled out your bra," Bridget said and grabbed Kayleigh's hands. She pulled her off the step and held Kayleigh's arms out wide to gaze down at her chest.

"Oh, you're hysterical." Kayleigh snuck a peek at her small chest and Bridget's much rounder one before pulling her arms down and crossing them across her body.

"Loosen up, Kay. You should celebrate the girls and wear something sexy!"

"I don't think fifteen and sexy should go together," she countered.

"I would agree," her father said, coming into the foyer with another box of decorations, "although I'm not sure what we're talking about."

"Oh, nothing, Dad," Kayleigh said and jumped up from the step, turning a deep shade of mortified.

"Just girl stuff, *Don* Cedro," Bridget said. "And I have to be going now, anyway. Kayleigh, I'll see you later to try on our non-sexy costumes." She smiled and waved at them both on her way out the door.

Kayleigh sighed and looked at her father, waiting for the lecture. He appeared concerned and finally set the box down. He slowly sat in a clover green accent chair. Lines of sorrow marred his face.

"I'm sorry you don't have your mom here for girl stuff."

"What?" Kayleigh said, surprised it wasn't the lecture she was expecting.

"You must have endless questions about...things, and I'm not the best person to help you make sense of it all," he said.

"It's okay, really," Kayleigh said, "I've already figured out most of the big stuff, and there's always the Internet."

Her father winced. "Doesn't make me feel any better. There is tons of misinformation on the Internet."

"Then, I can ask questions in health class with Mr. Rhodes—wait, maybe not there." She frowned. "I'm sure Nurse Rouhani would provide an educated female perspective if I needed it."

"Ah, yes, Soraya can be quite helpful," he said, and his face seemed to soften. He looked off into the distance, and a small smile played at the corner of his mouth

"Or Mrs. O'Neill," Kayleigh said quickly, frowning at her father. She disliked the idea that he was thinking about Mrs. Rouhani as more than just the school nurse. "Mrs. O'Neill is a woman, too. Right next door and older. She is probably a wealth of information on all kinds of things."

"Huh? Mrs. O'Neill? Yes, I'm sure she is," he said and stood. "I'd better be finishing dinner."

Once her father left, Kayleigh hung the rest of the Halloween décor. She picked up the colorful Day of the Dead mask and admired its bold blue, yellow, and red designs. Lifting it to her face, she surveyed the front hallway through its round, hollow eyes. She imagined having long black hair, brown skin, and dark, exotic eyes. A shiver ran across the back of her head and down her neck. It was suddenly several degrees warmer, and her hair seemed to slide off her shoulder and down the length of her arm. She peered through the mask at a dark lock of hair cascading as far as her elbow.

"What the...?" She pulled the mask away from her face and studied her hair. It was her color, brick red-brown, frizzy, and messy. "Yikes, some imagination you've got there, Kayleigh," she said to herself.

She joined her father at the dinner table, and they ate in silence.

Friday after school, Bridget came back with the costumes to get dressed for the dance. She wouldn't tell Kayleigh what she had picked out for them. She said, "Just trust me."

Kayleigh wondered about whether or not to tell Bridget about what she had seen. "Hey, Bridget?" she asked, while Bridget was changing into her costume.

"Yeah," Bridget said, her voice muffled from behind the bathroom door.

"Have you ever had strange feelings in your body, like you can feel goose bumps or shivers all over?"

"Yeah, when I think about Nathan Arscott." Bridget giggled.

Kayleigh thought about Nate, wearing his new junior high lacrosse jersey and tight athletic shorts. Mmm. She shook her head of that image and mentally scolded herself. "Nice, but no, that wasn't what I was referring to."

"So are we talking about your *diddies* again, then?" Bridget said.

"No, not those either," she said, glancing down at her breasts. "I was just wondering about normal changes in the body and then...other changes."

"I have no idea what you mean." Bridget said, opening the bathroom door, "but wait until you change into this costume." She came out holding a large garment bag and handed it to Kayleigh. Then, she twirled.

Bridget was dressed as a black swan, with a sleeveless black leotard trimmed in black feathers, a fluffy black tutu, large silky black wings, and a feathered headdress. She had painted her face white with dramatic black eye makeup in the shape of two feathers, and her lips were dark red. Two long black gloves had plumes of feathers by the elbows, and black ballet slippers adorned her feet.

"What do you think?" Bridget asked.

"Uh, my costume better not look like yours," Kayleigh said.

"What does that mean?" She put one hand on her hip.

"I mean you look gorgeous, but there is no way I will pull off a look like that. I can see the outline of your whole body."

"I know. Isn't it great?" Bridget pirouetted again, this time *en pointe*.

"Great for you, maybe, but not for me. Your host family may not keep many tabs on you, but there is no way my dad will let me out of the house with that on."

"You could always tell him you're sick, then sneak out," Bridget said. She motioned to the bay window, where Emilio lay sleeping on the bench seat.

Kayleigh gazed out the window at the large white oak. "I'd rather have a costume I don't have to hide."

"So relax, then." Bridget unzipped Kayleigh's garment bag. "Lucky for you, your costume is different." She pulled out a long white dress with a fitted bodice of white feathers, a long skirt with layers of tulle and feathers, and large white wings. "You're the white swan."

"Oh, you're kidding. That's not much better!" Kayleigh groaned and fell back on the bed, covering her face with her hands.

"You baby. It has far more material than mine," Bridget said, pulling out the matching white tights and white slippers. "And naturally the white swan is far more innocent. You'll look amazing!"

Kayleigh just groaned again and rolled her eyes. "No way am I wearing that"

"Try it on," Bridget said, yanking her off the bed. "Try it on first and then you can make a decision."

Kayleigh went into the bathroom and took off her clothes. She pulled on the tights and hesitantly slipped the dress over her head. Although strapless, a row of feathers at the top of the dress covered her chest, and the skirt fell to below her knees. It didn't seem as revealing as Bridget's version. She came out and faced Bridget. "Okay, this isn't so bad."

"Wait," Bridget said. She laced up the back of the bodice and attached Kayleigh's wings. The corset was snug around her middle but fanned out around her hips. "And the best part," Bridget said, and placed a silver tiara on Kayleigh's head. In the center of the intricate swirls of the tiara was the silhouette of a swan, accented with tiny sparkling stones and a shiny black eye.

Bridget sat Kayleigh on the bed and pulled out a makeup kit. For the next twenty minutes, Kayleigh fidgeted and played with the feathers on her dress as various brushes glided along her face. Bridget finally grinned and gestured toward the mirror. Kayleigh's eyes widened as she beheld her friend's art. Delicate wings of white paint fanned out from each of her eyes, swooped up around to her forehead and down her cheek. Her eyes were rimmed with sparkling white liner, and her lips were painted a rosy pink. Kayleigh stood in front of the mirror and marveled at how different she looked.

"Perfect," Bridget said and stood next to Kayleigh. "Now, who doesn't feel like an entirely different person? You could be Odette and I Odile."

"Doesn't Odile try to steal Odette's lover or something?" Kayleigh asked.

"Oh, don't be so literal." Bridget laughed. "They're beautiful costumes, and we'll have a great time."

"Yeah, but why swans?"

"Because swans are majestic and important animals," Bridget said, placing her hands on her hips. She looked at Kayleigh with a mixture of anger and impatience.

"Okay, jeez. I was just asking," Kayleigh said, although she wondered if it was coincidence that her mother and Bridget both liked swans. It was probably only an Irish thing.

Kayleigh's phone chose that moment to *beep beep*. She immediately felt a cold wave of apprehension steal over her as she tapped on the text.

Ben: wasup? w2m b4 dance?

Kayleigh sighed with relief. "It's Ben," she said to Bridget. "He wants to know if we want to meet up before the dance. I'll tell him we're on the way." She texted him.

Kayleigh: ok otw

Ben quickly texted back.

Ben: gr8! w8ing w/ frnds, cul.

"Ben says he's waiting for us with the others," Kayleigh relayed to Bridget. "We should go."

"Let me go to the *loo* before we leave," Bridget said, and disappeared into the bathroom.

Kayleigh started to put away her phone when another *beep beep* sounded. She wondered what else Ben wanted to tell her.

Anonymous: Don't you know Odette dies at the end?

Her heart leapt to her throat and skipped a beat.

It was not from Ben. The avatar was the same black circle that had appeared alongside the first text about not having a mother's shoulder to cry on.

"Bridget, look at this!" She yelled through the door.

Bridget came out, adjusting her skirt. "All right, hold your horses."

Kayleigh passed the phone to her friend, who reacted immediately.

"She's a blooming header, that Emma. What a load of bullocks." Her accent grew thicker as she got angrier. "Don't you pay any mind to her silly blather, Kayleigh." She threw the phone on the bed.

"Think about what she's saying, though. She must be able to see us!" Kayleigh rushed to the windows and drew the shade. "This doesn't seem like Emma, though. She's a pain, but she's not a stalker."

Beep beep! Both girls jumped and looked at the phone. Kayleigh slowly picked it up, looking at the window.

Ben: Wru???

She let out a long sigh. "It's Ben. Let's go."

Twenty minutes later, Kayleigh's father dropped them off in front of the school to meet their friends. "Have a good time," he said.

"What took you guys so long?" Ben asked. He was dressed as a wolf, but instead of looking scary, his mask looked more like Wile E. Coyote.

"I've got another secret admirer." Kayleigh handed the phone to Natalie. "Nat, can you figure out who sent it?"

Natalie took off her Pikachu hoodie and carried the phone to her bag. She pulled out a small laptop and connected the phone with a cable. As she typed, the furrow between her brows deepened.

"Now, are you ready to ask an adult for help?" Daiyu said and adjusted her blonde wig. "Emma has gone too far. She said you or Odette dies. Dead. That's a threat."

"The thing is, *Snow Queen*," Kayleigh said, glancing at Daiyu's princess dress, "I don't think it's Emma. She's mean, but I don't think she would threaten me. Or at least not with death. This feels like the same person who sent me the Nonys. Emma was in the cafeteria when those were sent, and she was busy shrieking over her missing Me3 page."

"Wow, they hid their tracks pretty well," Natalie said, looking up from her computer. "Theoretically, since these are only texts, they should be easy to trace, even if they used a dummy text program like Punt."

"What's Punt?" Kayleigh asked.

"It's a program you can use to text when you don't want the recipients to know your real phone number," Natalie said. "You usually have to put in some information to get the account, though, but when I trace the black circle, it comes up as a dead end. Not as in protected information. As in not there. No typical kid trying to be anonymous is that good. Plus, the way these were hidden seem similar to the Nonys. These had to be set up by pros."

"You mean professional hackers?" Daiyu asked. "As in adults?" Her mouth dropped open, and she wrung her hands. "Does anyone think maybe it's time to get other adults involved, then?"

"I agree with Daiyu," Martin said, dressed as a zombie football player. "It's time for some backup."

"Yeah, that makes sense," Kayleigh said. "It's the next level when someone is spying on me. Although—wait a minute! Guys, it still could be Emma. Doesn't her father work in computers?"

"He owns a couple of IT firms," Nat said.

"Well, we won't be able to do anything tonight," Bridget said, "so we might as well have some fun at the dance."

Kayleigh hesitated. Someone clearly didn't like her much at all, and now the person had threatened her life. Going into a crowded place didn't seem so wise. She took a breath and stifled the urge to run and hide. If it was Emma, she certainly knew how to ruin Kayleigh's night.

Kayleigh shook her head and exhaled. There was no reason to let anyone, especially not another fifteen-year-old girl, spoil her evening. She looked down at her costume, flipped her long auburn curls off her bare shoulders, and lifted her chin.

They entered the gymnasium into a sea of colorful costumes. A girl dressed as a swallowtail butterfly walked by, with two-feet-long yellow and blue wings floating behind her. Black and orange streamers twisted down from the ceiling, spider webs were sprayed into every corner, and someone had made a toilet paper mummy in a cardboard sarcophagus.

The sounds of chains and creaky doors played from a small speaker hidden behind the mummy.

Several students were already dancing to "Monster Mash," and at least four teachers circled the floor, ready to stop any twerking or other lewd moves.

"So, Kayleigh, you wanna dance?" Ben asked. He adjusted the partial mask over his face that gave him gray fur, black whiskers, and a pink nose. He held out one paw and gestured to the center of the gym.

Kayleigh didn't move. She wasn't a huge fan of dancing, and she didn't want to encourage Ben's crush.

"Ah, we barely got here," she said. "Maybe later."

His gaze fell to the floor, and he shrugged. "Yeah, okay, maybe later."

"Oh, look," Bridget said. "Emma already selected her first victim." She pointed to the throng of students.

Emma, dressed as Catwoman, tugged on Nathan's hand and pulled him into the middle of the dancers. She swayed back and forth, looking coyly from beneath her lashes.

Nathan, dressed completely in green, shuffled his slippered feet, although not in time with the music. A pointed felt hat with a feather sat upon his head, and a plastic sword swung from a brown belt.

A pang of jealousy stabbed through Kayleigh. Emma's skintight leather cat suit showed off her ample curves, and her makeup accented her eyes and lips. She moved closer to Nate and brushed against him, running her hand over his bicep.

He moved back out of her reach and pulled on his sleeve. He scanned the crowd, his eyes wide.

"Aw, poor Peter Pan's too much of a lost boy to handle Emma," Bridget said, clucking her tongue. "He needs to be rescued." Kayleigh watched as Bridget sauntered to them.

"*Oi*, Nate," she yelled over the music at him. "Mr. Constantine's looking for you. Come with me!" She grabbed his arm and pulled him away from Emma, who glared. She huffed and walked off the other way to find her next "victim."

Kayleigh winced at Nate being dragged off the dance floor, which didn't seem like much of a rescue. Neither girl should be manhandling him.

"Did I do something?" Nate asked.

"Nah, you're not actually wanted by the principal," Bridget said. She smiled and threw an arm over his shoulders. "I just thought you'd want out of that cat's claws."

A twinge of longing crept up Kayleigh's body as she watched Bridget lean into Nate.

"Emma? Oh, yeah, she can be a bit pushy." He took a step back from Bridget and looked at the rest of her entourage.

"You're safe here," Daiyu said, although her glance lingered on Bridget.

Nate shifted on his feet and hesitated. An awkward silence fell over them. Michael Jackson's "Thriller" came on, and kids lined up for the zombie dance.

Emma, Hannah, and Madison led the group as Catwoman, Poison Ivy, and The Joker's Daughter. They staggered rhythmically at the chorus and swung their arms from side to side. They moved their heads back and forth and clapped in unison.

"So, Nate," Martin said. "I hear you'll try out for the varsity lacrosse team in the fall."

"Possibly," he said. "Coach thinks I've grown enough on the rec league to skip JV."

"And grown, he has," Bridget whispered to Kayleigh. Kayleigh elbowed her friend in the side.

The music changed from "Thriller" to the slower "White Demon Love Song" by the Killers. Students paired up, and the movement in the gym slowed.

"Ben, would you like to dance?" Daiyu asked. She raised one shoulder, cocked her head, and gave him a small smile.

"Uh, sure." He hesitated and glanced at Kayleigh. She quickly looked away.

Natalie wandered to the punch bowl, joining the other wallflowers who suddenly needed a beverage.

Martin bowed to Bridget. "Milady, may I have the honor of a dance?" he asked.

Bridget frowned at Nathan and Kayleigh. She sighed and let Martin take her hand.

After they left, Kayleigh realized she was left standing alone with Nathan. Her stomach fluttered, and her palms grew slick.

"Well, Kayleigh, shall we?" Nathan asked. He brushed the blond hair off his forehead and adjusted his hat. He studied her, his blue-green eyes scanning her hair and tiara. He smiled.

Kayleigh smoothed her already well-combed tresses and placed a hand over her stomach. She took a breath and swallowed to ease the dryness in her throat.

She took his hand, and they slowly walked to the throng of students. Her palm stuck to his, which seemed equally warm and clammy.

He stopped in the middle of several couples and turned to Kayleigh. He placed his large hands lightly on her waist and moved close to her. He towered over her by several inches, which made her feel small and dainty. She rested her hands just below his broad shoulders.

She thought about her "bust" conversation with Bridget and looked down at her chest, wishing she were shapelier. She wondered how she could compete with girls like Emma and Bridget who filled out their bras.

That same, strange feverish sensation spread over her skin, and a shiver raced up her arms. The skin under Nathan's hands tingled. The bodice of her dress squeezed her rib cage, making it hard to breathe. She stopped dancing and gulped in air.

"Are you okay?" Nathan asked.

"I'm fine. I think Bridget laced up my dress too tight." The feathers lining the top of her dress suddenly bent outwards. Kayleigh watched in horror as her breasts grew out the top of the bodice, pushed aside the feathers, and formed deep cleavage.

Pop. One of the laces in the back of her dress broke, and she gasped. She looked at Nathan and crossed her arms over her chest. Warmth spread through her face, and her stomach flipped.

"Uh, I'm sorry, I've got…growing, ah…bathroom." She rushed off the dance floor, pushed past the students by the punch bowl, and launched herself into the girls' locker room.

The cool air washed over her as she entered the changing area, and she sagged against a locker. She took several deep breaths, her dress loosening with each lungful. She dared a look down and saw she had shrunk back to normal under the feathers. She crossed to one of the sinks and faced the mirrors.

A young woman with wide hazel eyes rimmed in white eyeliner stared back at her. Freckles stood out on an ashen face with scarlet cheeks. She ran a hand over the feathers on her top and studied the silver swan etched in the tiara. The swan looked graceful and elegant. Her mother loved swans, she thought.

Another shudder rolled over her, and her vision blurred. The strange sensation returned and ran through her extremities. Her scalp tingled, and her hair floated in the air. The auburn strands shrank, lifted off her shoulders, and lightened into bright white.

Her reflection in the mirror shimmered, and feathers replaced strands of hair. She reached up and touched a silky feather protruding from her scalp. In a swift motion, she yanked the feather from her head and yelped. A sharp sting jolted through her.

In the palm of her hand, she held not a white feather, but a chunk of a red-brown curl.

"What is happening to me?" she asked the empty locker room.

CHAPTER FOUR

THE MORPH

Kayleigh sat in her mother's sitting room at her small writing desk in front of the window. She gazed out at the backyard, elbow on the desk, and her chin propped up under one hand. Fat snowflakes drifted from a white blanket of sky and accumulated on the deck. Blackbirds flew from the bare trees to the bird feeders, fighting each other for safflower and sunflower seeds. The deep red of several male cardinals contrasted against the bright white snow. Squirrels chittered and searched for buried nuts. She lounged and watched the birds flutter back and forth, her mind blank and calm.

A red fox jumped out of the brush and lunged at a bird. Kayleigh jolted up, startled. Its fluffy tail twitched back and forth, and it jumped several times trying to catch a small sparrow. The birds all retreated to the safety of the trees, and the fox wandered back into the bushes.

Kayleigh slumped back on her desk. Her elbows rested on her history homework, which couldn't keep her attention. She dropped her head into her hands and rubbed her eyes. She wasn't sure if she could trust her vision.

Witnessing a fox hunting his breakfast probably ranked as ordinary. Pulling swan feathers out of your skull, however, was not so mundane. She touched the spot behind her ear, remembering how it had stung. Later it was discovered that someone had secretly spiked the punch, so although she didn't remember having any, she supposed being drunk could explain what she had seen. Perhaps alcohol caused hallucinations—she didn't have enough experience with it to know.

Several feet of snow had already fallen, although winter wouldn't officially begin for several weeks. This was due to the "lake effect" from Lake Ontario, where cool air moved over the warmer lake, picked up moisture, and dumped several feet of snow over the land to the south. This "snowbelt" stretched from Buffalo, New York, across her small town outside of Syracuse, and northward to Watertown.

The white powder sparked an old memory of her and her mother shoveling snow from the driveway. The plow had come by and made a snow bank over six feet tall, blocking them in. They shoveled for hours, stopping to throw snowballs, dig a tunnel, and make an igloo. The photo showed Kayleigh in pink winter gear, covered from head to toe, standing next to a pile of white twice her height.

Kayleigh smiled and looked back out at the winter wonderland. Her mother could make any situation fun, even shoveling snow. A dull ache lodged itself in the middle of her ribcage.

She surveyed her mother's sitting room, where Kayleigh kept her desk. The walls were lined with books, similar to her father's study, but rather than a heavy wood bureau, her mother had a small table, two lounge chairs, a love seat, and an ottoman. Kayleigh had loved when her mother would curl up in here with her and tell her stories.

A knock at the door broke her reverie. "Come in."

Her father entered with a small tray of cookies and hot chocolate. "*Hola, princesita,*" he said. "I thought you might like a snack. Are you getting any homework done?"

"Sorta. Ancient world history."

"Ah, good, so you can improve the D you got first quarter." He set the platter on an end table and sat on a chair patterned with peacock blues and emerald greens.

Kayleigh blushed and hung her head. The daughter of a history professor shouldn't struggle so much with that subject.

"History was your mother's favorite subject as well," he said. "Especially the ancient variety. She loved studying the chronicles of the British Isle."

"What is now England, Ireland, Scotland and Wales, right?" Kayleigh picked up the mug of hot chocolate and watched the heat rise off the liquid in curls of mist.

Her father nodded, rose and crossed to the bookshelves filled with James Joyce, Oscar Wilde, and Bram Stoker. "Her favorite book, in fact, was an anthology of Irish myths." He ran his index finger along the worn spines. He paused at a thick leather-bound volume and pulled it off the shelf.

"Myths aren't exactly history, Dad," Kayleigh said. She ate one of the shortbread cookies, buttery and rich.

"Your mom always believed these to be true. I saw that as her most whimsical quality." He smiled and looked out the window for a moment.

He handed Kayleigh the thick volume, which had "Irish Myths" in ornate letters embossed on the cover. She trailed her fingers over the smooth leather and traced the title. The first several pages were intricate drawings in colored inks of beautiful women with long flowing hair, lush landscapes, ravens, and swans.

"I remember this book," she said. "The evil stepmother turned the kids into swans." Kayleigh thought of the necklace. "They changed back into humans before the end, though, right?"

"Something like that." Her father smiled and took a cookie. "Well, I'll leave you to finish your history."

Her father left and closed the door to the study. The spicy scent of his aftershave lingered, mixing with the sweet smell of hot chocolate.

Kayleigh studied the book in her hands. The individual pages were sewn together, and she could see the stitching along the binding. The paper on the inside cover looked sealed to the leather. She flipped through and saw stories written by hand with fancy calligraphy.

The back cover felt thicker compared to the front. The edge of the paper covering the back end curled up, revealing the inside of the leather cover. A corner of a folded piece of violet paper stuck out of the back.

Kayleigh pulled it out and realized it was a piece of her mother's stationery. She unfolded the paper. It was dated on Kayleigh's birthday two years ago, the day her mother had disappeared.

My dearest Kayleigh,

I am writing this because I fear I may not be with you much longer. I would never leave you of my own free will, but there are complicated forces at work. I cannot be clearer without risk of putting you or your father in further danger.

Know that I love you very much, and you are turning into a beautiful young woman. Although it is sometimes painful, don't be afraid of growth. Enjoy each wonderful moment, for everything changes.

Take care of your father.

I love you,

Mom

Kayleigh swiped at the tears and sniffed several times, taking deep breaths to hold herself together. The fact that her mother knew something was happening but didn't tell her stung like betrayal.

Underneath the note was a thick piece of parchment paper folded in half. Kayleigh unfolded it to reveal a sketch of a swan sitting atop a key. She pulled the necklace from underneath her shirt and studied the pendant. Previously, her attention had been drawn to the swan about to take flight; she had assumed the key was decorative.

As she studied the drawing, she noticed the shape of the key — same round shaft, four jagged teeth — definitely the same key. So her mother did want her to have it and perhaps wanted her to open something with it. *But what did it open?*

Kayleigh reread the note several times, wondering about the "complicated forces" that prevented her from telling Kayleigh more about what was happening. She noticed her mother had written "further danger," which implied Kayleigh was already in danger. The nasty Nonys and Punts certainly made her feel threatened.

Goosebumps danced down her arms, and shivers rolled across her shoulders. As her apprehension grew, the walls of the once cozy sitting room closed in on her. In one fluid moment she leapt up and opened the door. Racing down the hall to her father's bedroom, she found him folding laundry. "Dad, look at this!"

He took the stationery and parchment and silently read for several moments. Kayleigh watched his eyebrows communicate like Morse code — jump with surprise, furrow with confusion, and lift together with grief. The hand holding the papers trembled.

"Where did you find this?"

"In Mom's book of Irish myths." Kayleigh placed a hand on her chest, where under her sweater the pendant cooled her skin and her heart thundered. She reached for the chain to pull the necklace out.

"We must give them to the police." Her father's voice seemed forced and tight, like the Hoover Dam straining to hold back the Colorado River.

Kayleigh's hand paused over the necklace. She had wanted to show it to her father from the moment it arrived, but something held her back. He would also want to turn it over to the police, but someone had clearly wanted her to have the necklace. Otherwise it already would have been given to the police. *Let them have the drawing instead.*

Her mother's lavender stationery fluttered in his hand as her father strode to the telephone to call the lead detective on her mother's case. A dull ache grew behind her eyes, and she rapidly blinked.

The pendant hung heavy around her neck, mirroring the guilt that hung heavy in her heart as she pondered who had sent her the key and what it unlocked. She sighed in frustration that each clue she found seemed to warrant more questions than it answered.

In the weeks that followed, Kayleigh obsessively searched for keyholes everywhere—on doors, cupboards, the armoire. The key could fit something halfway around the world for all she knew, but then why would someone have sent it to her? *You mother thinks you should have this.*

The police had forensics analyze her mother's note and the drawing of the key, but the lead detective said the information didn't bring any new clues. Her father explained, his voice wavering, that they suspected her mother was dead, although under New York state law an individual wasn't officially presumed dead until seven years had passed.

"Hey, Kayleigh...earth to Kayleigh...come in Kayleigh," her father said. His voice broke through her daydreaming.

"Huh?" She blinked, and the dining room came into focus.

"You're supposed to be setting the table for Thanksgiving." He motioned to the stack of china in front of where she sat in the dining room. There were gourds of various colors and sizes laid out as a centerpiece.

"Yeah, I know," she said. She glanced at the plates but didn't make any move towards arranging the place settings. It was her mother's favorite china, which pictured autumn leaves in bright colors. It still didn't seem right eating off her mother's favorite pattern without her.

Her father looked at her and their eyes met. He nodded.

"How about you go baste the turkey, instead?" her father asked.

"Sure," she answered and went into the kitchen. She grabbed the baster with one hand and slipped the other into a potholder. When she opened the oven, the warm scent of turkey and stuffing washed over her. She took a deep breath and identified sage, rosemary, and thyme. She used the baster to suction up some of the juices from the bottom of the pan and then drizzled them over the golden bird.

This would be the third year that Mrs. O'Neill joined them for Thanksgiving. The first year, just two months after her mother disappeared, she and her dad hadn't prepared for Thanksgiving. They both had sat in a fog of grief and let the day come. Mrs. O'Neill had knocked on the door that afternoon with a turkey casserole in her hands and brought Thanksgiving with her.

This year they had prepared all the typical trimmings, including sweet potatoes, stuffing, green beans, and cranberry sauce. Mrs. O'Neill had said she would bake an apple pie and a pumpkin pie.

Ding Dong. The front doorbell rang, and Kayleigh went through the family room to the entry. A ripple of excitement ran through her as she'd been waiting to ask her neighbor about the key. She pulled open the heavy oak door.

Mrs. O'Neill stood on the stoop, wrapped in a heavy cloak, scarf, and hat. She held a pie in each hand.

"Hello, Mrs. O'Neill," Kayleigh said. She took one of the pies. Heat radiated from the bottom of the glass dish, and the scents of pumpkin, nutmeg, and cinnamon tickled Kayleigh's nose.

"Happy Thanksgiving, dearie," Mrs. O'Neill said. She stepped into the foyer and took off her hat. Long silver hair spilled down her shoulders.

"Happy Thanksgiving," Kayleigh said. She kissed the elderly woman on her wrinkled cheek and hung her cloak and scarf on the coat tree. The edges of the swan pendant gently tickled her skin as she moved.

"Mrs. O'Neill, you know the package—"

"Happy Thanksgiving. We're so glad you could come," her father appeared from the living room, interrupting her. "Please, come sit down."

Kayleigh blew her bangs off her forehead and stifled her frustration.

Their elderly neighbor settled herself on a loveseat, embossed with red and gold threads. "Thank you for the invitation. It gives me a chance to check up on this gorgeous girl you have here." She gestured to Kayleigh. "How's school going, lass?"

A flicker of guilt poked at Kayleigh as she sat next to her neighbor. "Better, I guess, I'm trying to raise my history grade."

"Glad to hear it. History is so important."

"So I've been told." Kayleigh said. She pinched a lock of hair between her fingers and smoothed it behind her ear.

"You know," Mrs. O'Neill continued. "This region is full of immigrants from Ireland who can tell you about our history."

"Bridget tells me all the—Hey, do you know Bridget Byrne?"

Mrs. O'Neill frowned and tilted her head to one side. Her eyes closed, and her lips pursed.

Brrring. The kitchen timer went off. Kayleigh jumped. "The turkey must be ready," she said.

"I'll get it," Mrs. O'Neill said. She sprang off her seat and darted into the kitchen. Emilio followed, an orange feline blur, probably hoping she'd drop some on the floor.

"Wow, she certainly is spry for her age," Kayleigh said.

"I don't know where she gets her energy," her father said. "Come on. We'd better help her with all the food."

The three of them brought the turkey and side dishes into the dining room. The collection of small gourds spilling out of a woven basket in the middle of the table reminded Kayleigh of the Pilgrims.

"How nicely you set the table, Cedro," Mrs. O'Neill said.

"Thank you. Please, be seated." He held out her chair.

Kayleigh sat across from her neighbor, next to her father, who was at the head of the table.

"Shall we say grace?" Mrs. O'Neill asked.

"Oh, that would be nice," her father said. "We haven't been so formal since my wife…"

"That's quite all right, Cedro. You and Kayleigh have been through so much. You could use an extra blessing from Him." She pointed upwards and smiled. Then she bowed her head. "We give Thee thanks, Almighty God, for all Thy benefits and for the poor souls of the faithful departed, through the mercy of God."

Kayleigh shifted in her chair. Any mention of God made her want to change the topic.

"Also, please keep Cedro and Kayleigh safe," Mrs. O'Neill continued. "And watch over Órla, wherever she may be. Amen."

Kayleigh gaped at Mrs. O'Neill in surprise. She hadn't expected her to include her mother. Her father, however, looked at Mrs. O'Neill with a glimmer of tears in his eyes. "Thank you."

"You're welcome," she said and patted his hand.

Kayleigh ate dinner mostly in silence, while Mrs. O'Neill and her father made small talk about the weather, winterizing the pipes, and her plans for gardening in the springtime. Kayleigh conversed enough to appear polite and engaged in the conversation, but her mind was elsewhere.

Kayleigh thought about God and faith. It was hard for her to blindly accept that God had their best interests in mind. Being Catholic meant putting trust in the Father, the Son, and the Holy Ghost, but at times the three of them must be out to lunch—like the day her mother disappeared.

After dinner her father and Mrs. O'Neill sat in the living room drinking coffee, and Kayleigh excused herself. She had lost the desire to be thankful.

There were only three short weeks between Thanksgiving and Christmas break, and Kayleigh spent them studying hard to bring up her grades. The second quarter didn't end until mid-January, so Kayleigh couldn't afford to goof off for vacation and not study. One D, two C grades, and the rest Bs first quarter was not her most stellar work.

Kayleigh woke up early on Christmas morning and padded downstairs in her footy pajamas. She curled up on the sofa with a fleece blanket and gazed at the tree she and her father had decorated. The colored lights twinkled and shone among the pine needles. Red, green, blue, and purple lights bounced off ornate gold balls, sending rays of color among the branches. Little Santas, wooden elves, and reindeer danced among the strings of popcorn and candy canes.

Outside, the snow continued to fall, and a fresh blanket of white covered the road. The sun had barely begun to peek through the clouds, and birds chirped in the trees. A snowplow rumbled up the street.

Kayleigh liked the quiet of early morning. Before the world woke up, she felt peaceful. She could pretend that both her parents were asleep upstairs. Emilio crept across the sofa and settled in her lap. He purred as she stroked his soft fur.

She surveyed the packages under the tree and smiled. Her father had put several out after she had gone to bed, and she knew he would sign them "From Santa." She searched for them among the wrapping paper and boxes. But over in the corner, she spied an unwrapped gift—something made of wood beneath the tree.

Curious, she pushed the cat off her lap and unearthed the present from its neighbors. She pushed aside several brightly wrapped boxes and reached under the tree. Her fingers connected with curved wood. She found an edge and pulled the object towards her.

It was a small chest made of a dark wood, ornately carved with Celtic knots—similar to her jewelry box. Only this box had a curved top and a keyhole.

She pulled the necklace out of the top of her pajamas and took it off her neck. She held it up and examined the key pendant dangling off the chain. It seemed to be the right size. She took a deep breath and slid the key in the keyhole.

"Oh, you're awake," her father said from the door.

She yelled, startled. The key jerked back out of the lock and Kayleigh jumped up, palming the necklace. "Dad, you scared me."

"Sorry about that." He crossed over and hugged her. "Merry Christmas."

"Merry Christmas." The soft flannel of his robe warmed her cheek.

She waited as her father studied the brightly colored tree and smiled.

"Who brought over this chest?" she asked. She attempted to sound casual.

"Mrs. O'Neill, I think," he said. "She stopped by yesterday." He looked at her with a frown. "*¿Estas bien, mi princesita?*"

"I'm okay," she said. "Maybe I'm just hungry."

"I'll start the pancakes, then." He paused and looked again at her.

She held her breath and tried to look natural until he turned towards the kitchen.

Once the thud of the kitchen door echoed through the first floor, she turned her attention back to the chest, confident he was gone.

She knelt in front of the tiny trunk and took a deep breath. She slipped the key into the lock and turned it. With a soft *click*, the lid popped up. Kayleigh peered in at a sliver of the contents inside.

She placed one hand on the lid and questions swirled in her mind. The key had arrived through the postal service, or so said Mrs. O'Neill, but without a return address. The chest may or may not have been brought by Mrs. O'Neill, but the key opened it. She must get her elderly neighbor, who clearly knew more than she was letting on, alone.

Kayleigh opened the lid and her fingers brushed the soft felt lining. Several documents lay in a stack on a small tray at the top of the compartment. She pulled out the first paper to find another note written on her mother's violet stationery.

Kayleigh, if you are reading this note, then it is finally time for you to have this chest. I am so proud you have begun "The Change." These items will illuminate for you this wonderful Morphosis. Love, Mom.

Underneath the note, Kayleigh found a drawing in colored inks, which reminded her of the illuminated manuscripts of the middle ages. It pictured a woman with long flowing hair and a voluminous gown. She stood at the edge of a lake. The woman's eyes squinted, the bridge of her nose was crinkled, and her mouth turned down in anger.

She held out one hand, and swirls of colors seemed to float outward from the ends of her fingers and surround four forms. The first was a young girl, who recoiled from the woman in fear. The second, a boy, who clung to the girl. Next to the children sat a third shape that looked like half of a boy. His head and upper body looked human, but wings branched out from his torso, and from the waist down his body was feathered, and he had webbed feet. At the end of the lake sat a large white swan with a black and orange beak. It appeared the woman was turning the children into swans.

Under the image, someone had written a caption in calligraphy.

The first Irish shape-shifters.

From reading her mother's book of myths, Kayleigh knew the drawing portrayed the ancient Irish myth of "The Children of Lir." Aoife grew jealous of her stepchildren and cursed them to live as swans for 900 years. Versions of the story differed in what happened to them during those years, but most had the children turning back into humans, albeit elderly ones, at the end.

Kayleigh thought about Halloween night, when her hair had changed into feathers. Maybe it wasn't a hallucination due to alcohol! Her breathing quickened as she clutched at the drawing. Her hands trembled, her palms becoming clammy. The air thinned as she struggled to breathe, and her stomach turned to knots as she considered the idea that she had actually started to change into a swan.

Kayleigh set the picture aside, reached down, and pinched the corners of the tray. She lifted the shelf out of the chest, her hands shaking, threatening to drop it. She set the top compartment next to her on the rug and took in another ragged breath. She paused and listened for signs her father might come back.

In the lower compartment, she found a pair of reading glasses shaped like half-moons and a small leather-bound journal written in another language, probably Irish Gaelic. The only words she recognized were "Órla Aobh Purcell" scribbled on the inside cover.

She remembered the first time she read her mother's middle name, Aobh, as Ay-obe. Her mother had giggled, the sound of her laughter floating in the air. "It's an Irish name pronounced like Eve," she had said, and snatched up five-year-old Kayleigh for a hug.

Kayleigh blinked away tears, and a dull ache lodged in her chest.

At the bottom of the trunk was a scroll of some kind of thin leather wrapped with a chord of the same material. She gently unrolled it and revealed a large genealogy tree. Scrawled across the top in large letters was the word "Morphs." Four names stood out at the crown of the tree: Fionnuala, Aodh, Fiacra, Conn. The symbol for females accompanied the first, and the symbol for males marked the next three names. All four had the last name of "Lir." Lines and names forked off of each. They were marked with gender symbols and snaked down the page in intricate stems and branches.

At the bottom, Kayleigh saw her mother's name in tiny script. Underneath someone had written in thicker ink, "Katherine Leigh Paz-Purcell."

Kayleigh scanned back and forth from the Children of Lir at the top to her own name at the bottom, struggling to keep the many appellations straight. In the legend, King Lir and his wife, Aobh, had given birth first to a girl and a boy, Fionnuala and Aodh (meaning "fiery") and then two boys, Fiacra and Conn. When Aobh died in childbirth, Lir married her sister Aoife, the woman who grew jealous and turned her stepchildren into swans.

Kayleigh followed the intricate symbols and connections on the scroll that indicated all four children had children of their own. The genogram outlined generations of a family tree that spanned thousands of years — of which she was a part.

Beads of sweat formed on her brow, and her breathing quickened.

She reread her mother's note, thinking again about "The Change" and "wonderful Morphosis." She contemplated the myth — or maybe — reality, of the Children of Lir. Kayleigh allowed the terms to circle around in her head. Change. Morphosis. Metamorphosis. Shape-shifters. Morph.

"I am a morph," she said aloud. A wave of dizziness washed over her, and she rocked back onto her heels. Nausea rolled in her stomach, and acid crept up the back of her throat.

Kayleigh let the weight of those words sink into her head and down into her subconscious. Somehow she had already known that she was different, maybe even special. Never could she have guessed, however, that she was a morph, a shape-shifter.

Every time that strange flush spread across her skin, she was in the process of shifting forms. She had changed the color of her hair thinking about the Day of the Dead, and the night of the Halloween dance she had indeed started to become a swan. She'd even filled out her bodice with a mere wish.

Kayleigh sat back on her heels and took a deep breath. Puberty wreaked enough havoc on her body without adding another metamorphosis. She let out a small laugh as a tear escaped her eye and rolled down her cheek. The note her mother had hidden in the back of the book encouraged her to embrace changes as a natural part of life. And supernatural, it seemed.

Everything changes.

CHAPTER FIVE
TRAUMA

"Everything changes?" Bridget asked. "And you're a shape-shifter?" As she read the letter aloud her face revealed her skepticism—eyebrows drawn together, lips pursed, nose wrinkled.

"A morph." She and Bridget sat on her bed, looking at her mother's note. She'd called Bridget immediately after discovering the chest and begged her to come. Kayleigh knew how crazy it sounded, but she needed her friend's affirmation and support.

Bridget frowned at Kayleigh and reread the note. "I don't know, Kay. It sounds pretty cryptic. So you found this in her book?"

"Uh-huh, and then I found the other stuff in the chest."

"A journal in Gaelic, some reading glasses, and another vague note about a wonderful metamorphosis and 'The Change.' How do you know she wasn't talking about getting your period?" Bridget raised one eyebrow.

"Morphosis...and you're not funny." Kayleigh groaned, frustrated that Bridget wasn't taking her seriously. She was already confused enough, and she needed Bridget's help to clarify things. So far, her best friend wasn't helping.

Kayleigh opened the chest and took out the documents. She handed Bridget the drawing of Aoife transforming the children into swans.

"You're Irish, Bridget, so don't you remember the story of the Children of Lir?" Kayleigh asked.

"Of course. It was a bedtime story my grandmother used to tell me," Bridget said. "Nobody actually believed they were real, though. The story definitely didn't end with people being shape-shifters."

"Morphs. And we don't really know exactly what happened in those 900 years. That part of the story is fuzzy, no matter what version you read. What if the swans could mate?"

"With each other?" Bridget asked. "Ew, that would be incest."

"I meant with other swans, not each other."

"Then, there would be more swans," Bridget rolled her eyes. "Not more people."

"Swans that could turn into people, though," Kayleigh insisted.

"But wouldn't they mainly be swans?" Bridget asked. "Hatched from eggs? You're still mainly human."

"Obviously." Kayleigh flopped back on the bed and sighed. "On Halloween, though, when we dressed as swans, I pulled a feather out of my hair."

"Your costume was covered in feathers," Bridget said.

"I mean that when I pulled the feather, I pulled my hair," Kayleigh said. Bridget still shook her head. "I mean, since my hair had turned into the feather, I ripped hair out of my scalp when I yanked out the feather."

"Hair, feather, feather, hair. Kayleigh, you're not making much sense."

Kayleigh grabbed the scroll. "What about this genealogy?" She pointed to her name at the bottom.

Bridget waved her hand and snorted. "Right, some drawing of a tree that says you are in a family of morphs or shape-shifters or whatever." She cleared her throat. "I dunno. It seems pretty far-fetched."

"I know it does, but I've been having these weird feelings, like my skin is moving, or tingling."

Bridget grinned at Kayleigh. "There's a medical name for that, actually, I saw it on the Discovery Channel. It's called 'formication,' when you feel ants crawling on your skin." She leaned over and walked her fingers up Kayleigh's arm like bugs' feet.

"Ugh, get off." Kayleigh shuddered. "Don't be a smart-ass. It's not a medical condition, or at least I don't think so." She frowned and studied the skin on her arm. "I think I can feel every inch of my skin now because I can shift its shape," Kayleigh said.

"Hmm...feeling every inch of your skin could be nice if you're thinking about Nate," Bridget said. She waggled a finger at Kayleigh and made kissing sounds.

"Bridget, stop." She picked up a pillow and threw it at her friend.

"I'm just saying," Bridget said. "You've got a little crush. It was all over your face when you danced with him. Tall, blond, smart—who wouldn't find that appealing? Yet you don't do anything about it."

"Like what?" Kayleigh asked.

"Ask him out. Be assertive and get what you want," Bridget said.

"That's not me." Kayleigh crossed her hands in front of her body, remembering how she busted out of her dress when she danced with Nathan. The story lingered on the tip of her tongue, but embarrassment outweighed her desire to tell Bridget.

"So...you're not going to make the first move with Nathan, fine," Bridget said. "What about when you stand there and let Emma walk all over you?"

"That's not exactly true," Kayleigh protested.

"Well, from where I stand, you're not doing much about that situation either, and now you're saying you're a morph because of some fiction you found in your mother's chest."

"It's not fiction. Maybe the story was written because the ability is real."

"That sounds pretty nuts, but okay, if you are a morph, let's see it," Bridget said.

"What?" Kayleigh asked. She sat up on the bed, surprised.

"Rather than blathering on about morphing, let's see you do it. Less talking, more doing."

"No way. I can't control it at all. I have no idea what I might change into." Kayleigh rubbed her hands over her forearms, a chill racing over her shoulders. "Even if I could change into anyone or anything, doesn't mean I should."

"So what are you planning on doing, then?" Bridget rose and held out her arms, hands palms down. "Wait around until you change into something and fly away?" She flapped her arms and stuck out her tongue.

A sinking sensation pulled at Kayleigh's stomach. "I don't know. I thought I'd start by telling you, but I don't think you believe me." She got up from where she was sitting on the bed and paced.

This conversation wasn't going as planned. Kayleigh had imagined her best friend reacting with surprise and pleasure, not sarcasm and disbelief. She needed someone to help her figure out the clues to being a morph, not to suggest she was having delusions. Loneliness crept over her and gnawed at her gut.

She caught sight of herself in the mirror. Her hair lay in tangles around her face, and the light glinted off the tears in her eyes. Gray shadows darkened the skin beneath each eye. She walked to the mirror, brushed a hand through her hair, sniffed, and dried her eyes with her sleeve.

Bridget slid off the bed and joined her, facing their images. "Your story is hard to buy, Kayleigh. But you're my best friend, so I'll love you no matter what." Bridget put an arm around her shoulders and gave her a squeeze.

Kayleigh surveyed the two of them. When she looked at Bridget, she saw a young woman. Bridget was several inches taller, a few cup sizes larger, sophisticated, and confident. Her long black hair cascaded in perfect waves over her shoulders, never a strand out of place. Those intense blue eyes rimmed in dark black lashes bewitched the unsuspecting male, and blemishes never tarnished her ivory skin.

Looking at herself, on the other hand, Kayleigh saw a girl, not a woman. Her russet hair frizzed on either side of her head, and freckles in various shades of brown peppered her skin, especially across her nose and cheeks. Her eyes, still a shade between brown and green, were certainly not alluring. She touched a zit that had formed on the side of her nose and groaned.

"Oh, forget those little nuisances," Bridget said, and brushed Kayleigh's finger away from her face. "One zit does not take away from the cuteness that is you." Bridget spoke in a baby voice and poked Kayleigh's dimples with her index fingers.

"That's easy for you to say when you look perfect," Kayleigh batted away Bridget's hands and turned to look again in the mirror. "Look at yourself. How do you think it is for me to have a supermodel as my best friend?"

Bridget's smile faded as she looked at her reflection. Eyes narrowed, her hand fluttered to her hair. Her eyes roamed over her body, and she took one hand and smoothed her skirt over her hip. Kayleigh thought she saw tears forming, but Bridget quickly took a breath. Kayleigh frowned, not sure how Bridget could be unhappy with her appearance.

Bridget crossed back to the bed and picked up the scroll. She handed it to Kayleigh.

"Whatever you believe, Kayleigh, I want you to fight for it. If you're a morph, then start morphing. If you like Nate, then go for it. If Emma's a mega-you-know-what to you, shut her down."

Ribbons of fear ran through Kayleigh's chest as Bridget spoke. She imagined standing up to Emma, telling her to leave her alone, but even in her own mind the words came out as pathetic. All Emma did was laugh and continue to insult her, which made Kayleigh want to bury her head in the sand.

Bridget laid the scroll on the bed and went to the door. "I've gotta get moving," she said. "My host family has some sort of special Christmas dinner planned for tonight."

"Oh, okay," Kayleigh said.

"Since they've been so kind to let me stay with them to study here in the U.S., I kinda owe it to them."

"Of course, I get it." Kayleigh wondered what it would be like to study in another country. So far away from friends and family, it must get lonely.

"Remember we're meeting up with Daiyu and Ben this weekend to review for midterms," Bridget said.

"Vacation's not even over," Kayleigh said.

"Daiyu's idea, not mine." Bridget smiled and shrugged her shoulders. "*Slán.*" She said goodbye in Irish Gaelic.

"*Adios.*" Kayleigh responded in Spanish.

Kayleigh stared at the door long after Bridget had left. Inklings of doubt began to crawl their way back into her brain. After finding the chest, she was so sure she was a morph. Bridget seemed to find the whole thing preposterous, though. Kayleigh certainly couldn't produce any proof.

Kayleigh wandered to the bed and picked up the papers. She reread her mother's notes, and pangs of longing filled her chest. If only her mother were there and could straighten everything out. Drawings and cryptic notes made everything more confusing.

She traced an index finger over her name at the bottom of the family tree. *Katherine Leigh Paz-Purcell.* It seemed foreign to her, like it belonged to someone she didn't recognize. Her vision blurred, and tears trickled down her cheeks.

She folded the papers and shoved them back in the chest along with the glasses. After the lock clicked shut, she looped the necklace once again around her neck and slid the chest underneath her bed.

Enough obsessing over fantastical ideas. She pushed aside her thoughts about being a morph and turned her attention to midterms. Morphing was still optional, but flunking 9th grade was not.

Six weeks later, Kayleigh sat in the lunchroom with her friends and ate her sandwich. Voices, the clinking of silverware, and a low whir of machines from the kitchen blurred into white noise. She'd made it through midterms, and she had managed to earn straight B grades. Hopefully, that would help bring up her overall GPA.

"What if we all met up at the movies? That's not as date-like," Ben said.

"What's not as date-like?" Kayleigh asked, coming out of her thoughts to catch part of the conversation.

"If we met at the movies as a group," Daiyu said. She looked as disappointed as if she'd gotten an A minus on a paper.

"Pay attention, Kayleigh. Saturday is Valentine's Day," Bridget said. "Our Martin is having problems deciding whether to meet Hannah at the movies or pick her up." She threw an arm around Martin, whose face looked as red as the tomato sauce on his ravioli.

"Hannah?" Kayleigh asked. "As in...Emma's BFF?"

Martin shrugged and looked down at his pasta. "She asked me to take her to the movies, and before I knew what was happening, I agreed to go."

"That's why we're trying to figure out how to make it less of a date. It's more casual if he meets her there," Ben said.

"I get casual, but not Hannah," Kayleigh said.

"So what's the problem, other than she's a spawn of Satan?" Natalie asked. She looked up from her computer, winked at Kayleigh, and wrinkled her nose at Martin.

"She's not as mean as Emma," Bridget said. "She does stand there and let her friend trash us, but maybe we shouldn't judge her based on the company she keeps."

"She's all right, I guess," Martin said.

"All right?" Ben asked. "Hannah may be high maintenance, but she's beautiful."

As Ben spoke, Daiyu lowered her head and brushed her bangs out of her eyes.

"Since when did you care about appearances?" Bridget asked Ben. She raked her eyes up and down his short frame until he blushed and looked away.

"She's not my type," Martin said. He frowned and shook his head.

"So what are we debating, whether or not Martin should go to the movies with Hannah, or how to make it less of a date?" Kayleigh asked.

"I kinda already said yes, but I'll tell her I'll meet her there," Martin said. "And you guys come, too, so it'll be like a group thing."

"We'll back you up," Natalie said. She offered him a fist bump and went back to typing.

"So then we'll all meet you there," Ben said. "Casual like." He glanced at Daiyu, who was staring into her vegetables.

"Go where?" Nathan asked, arriving at their table.

Kayleigh's heart skipped a beat. She looked up to see him staring at her. He smiled, and butterflies took flight in her belly.

"The movies," Bridget said. She strolled next to Nathan and slid an arm around his shoulders. "It's a group date. Wanna come?"

Nathan continued to stare at Kayleigh. "Sure, I'll join you," he said.

The bell rang, and Kayleigh stood, grabbing her backpack. She followed the students who filed out of the cafeteria. Kayleigh glanced over her shoulder at Nathan, who was walking with Martin.

To occupy herself and reduce the rising blush in her cheeks, she scanned the hallway. Their school was built in the 1950s and had only been renovated once, so it wasn't open or spacious. Instead it made Kayleigh feel like a rat trapped in a maze. It had a grid of tight corridors, lined with lockers, and rooms were arranged in pods connected to each other in the center by doors. Classrooms had several doors, but no windows. The connecting accordion walls could be opened to make larger spaces, but even the classrooms next to the outside walls didn't have windows. The official word was the architects wanted to reduce heating costs, but Kayleigh thought they really wanted to cut down on distractions.

Kayleigh once had a dream where she was in class and had to give an oral report. During the middle of the presentation, a rush of panic engulfed her, and she lost the ability to speak. All she could make were squawking sounds, and the students around her howled with laughter. She ran to a nearby door, but it only led to another classroom full of students. They also started laughing at her. Through door after door, into classrooms she ran, her heart racing, head spinning, until she woke up drenched in sweat.

She frowned to bring herself out of the memory. The rush of chatter in the hallway roared around her.

Annoyed with herself, she pushed her way through students to English class. There was a distinct disadvantage to being only five feet tall when in a throng of students.

Kayleigh paused to wait for a student using his locker. With the locker door open and his backpack on the floor, there was not enough room to pass. He finished putting his books in his bag and closed the door. Instead of moving forward, though, he swung his bag back towards Kayleigh.

She tried to take a step back and yelped as the bag of books slammed into her shoulder. She lost her balance and tripped over her feet. She braced herself to hit the deck.

An arm slid around her waist and a palm grabbed her elbow to steady her. The weight of her upper body sagged against a muscled chest. A jolt of electricity stunned her shoulder where this new body connected with hers.

"Hey, watch it," a male voice called out to the student with the backpack. Bag boy glanced back at them, shrugged, and went on his way.

Kayleigh strained her head, trying to sneak a peek at her rescuer's face.

"Are you all right?" the boy asked. He lifted her to her feet, his bronze arm still circling her waist. His large, tawny hand spanned her rib cage and rested directly under the edge of her bra.

She pulled away, embarrassed. She brushed off her shirt and took a deep breath before she dared look at his face. She recognized him as another freshman she'd seen around but didn't know his name. His eyes, the same shade of light brown as his skin, focused on Kayleigh. She felt another shock travel through her body, but she couldn't place its source.

"Sorry about that. Some guys are jerks. You all right?" he repeated.

"Yeah, I'm okay," Kayleigh tried to laugh off her embarrassment. "Guys don't realize a bag full of books is a deadly weapon."

"Most definitely. Travel in the hallways at your own risk." He smiled and walked off.

Kayleigh watched him leave, suddenly a little grateful to have been hit with a bag of books, but the corridor emptied. She hurried to her class before the late bell rang.

She got to English and felt her phone vibrate. She had turned the ringer off during lunch, not willing to risk reading more Nonys in the busy cafeteria. She could ignore them if she never read them.

She sat at a desk and fished her phone out of her backpack.

Nate: Martin gave me ur number. c2c?

Her heart beat faster, and she smiled to herself. She couldn't believe Nate had asked if she cared to chat. Her English teacher started writing an assignment on the board. Kayleigh hid her phone underneath her desk.

Kayleigh: sure. Wasup?

Nate: biology

Kayleigh smiled and imagined Nate sitting in the science lab.

Kayleigh: English

Nate: r u going 2 movies sat?

Kayleigh sat up straight and looked at her phone. Nate had told her friends he would join them on Saturday. He asked her if she was going. Her thumbs hovered over the phone, and several responses raced through her mind.

Kayleigh: m/b

Well, that was brilliant. She slapped a palm to her forehead and groaned. "Maybe" didn't really answer his question. Bridget waved at her and put a finger to her lips. The teacher turned around and scanned the students. Kayleigh pretended to read *Much Ado About Nothing.*

When the teacher turned back to the board, Kayleigh got Bridget's attention. She pointed to the phone and mouthed the word "Nate."

Bridget smiled and nodded. Kayleigh's phone vibrated again.

Nate: I wanna c the new action flick, wau?

What about me? Kayleigh glanced at the other students, hoping they couldn't see her texting. Heat rose in her cheeks. He wanted to see the new action movie, something about a computer virus that shuts down the government. He still wasn't directly asking her to go with him, but she couldn't merely say maybe again.

Kayleigh: sounds interesting

Nate: w2m@7?

Now he did ask her to meet him—at 7 o'clock. Her heart raced, and her hands became sweaty. She wiped away the condensation on the phone with her sleeve. Her thumbs trembled as she decided what to type next.

Kayleigh: k

Kayleigh rolled her eyes and blew the hair out of her face. Wow, what an answer. "Okay" was barely a step above maybe.

Nate: mmt?

Her mouth grew dry, and she licked her lips. He wanted her to meet him there, so maybe this wasn't a date. She hesitated and texted her answer.

Kayleigh: k

Nate: gr8! it's a date.

Kayleigh dropped the phone into her bag and dragged air into her lungs. She had agreed to meet Nate at the movies, and he had called it a date. Her head felt light, and her skin quivered.

She put her head down on her Shakespeare book and whispered to herself. "Oh, no, don't turn into a swan again. Wait, don't think about swans, or you'll change. Stop. Don't think about morphing at all. Think about dating. No, not dating, either. Remember what happened last time you were with Nate. Think about—"

"Kayleigh?" The English teacher, Mrs. Williams, put a hand on her shoulder.

Kayleigh looked up at Mrs. Williams, who stood next to her desk.

The teacher frowned. "Are you okay?"

Kayleigh looked around the room and realized the class stared at her. Her face flushed, and she wanted to crawl into a hole.

"Do you need to go to the nurse?" Mrs. Williams asked.

"Uh, yeah. Maybe I'm not feeling well," she said.

She gathered her books and stepped out into the hall. She took a few steps down the corridor towards the nurse's office and sagged against a locker. Thoughts swirled around her head like a tornado.

Kayleigh closed her eyes and listened to the hum of voices in the classrooms. In the background, heat blew through the vents with a soft *whoosh*, and several doors opened and closed. Her breathing became steady, and a calm settled over her body. Her mind quieted. She imagined herself running in the snow, and she heard her mother laughing.

"Kayleigh?" Mr. Constantine broke her concentration. A tall and grim man, he presided over Onondaga High School with a firm hand. "Shouldn't you be in class?"

"Mrs. Williams sent me to the nurse," Kayleigh said. "Sorry, I'll get going." She scurried off and snuck a glance back at the principal. He stood in the middle of the corridor, not moving, still staring at her. She turned back and quickened her pace. She remembered the day last year when the eighth graders visited Onondaga for an orientation, and his somber vibe had made her very nervous. Her apprehension only intensified with every subsequent meeting.

She opened the door to the nurse's office and caught the faint smell of pistachios. Mrs. Rouhani sat by the window, back to the door.

"Hello, Mrs. Rouhani," Kayleigh said.

The nurse turned. Her mouth still full, she held up one finger.

"Oh, sorry, I didn't mean to interrupt your lunch."

Mrs. Rouhani finished chewing and wiped her mouth with an embroidered handkerchief. "I'm having dessert. Persian baklava from my country of Iran."

"It smells nice."

"It has almonds, pistachios, cardamom, and a rose-water syrup." Mrs. Rouhani rose and gestured for Kayleigh to sit on the cot. "When I smell pistachios, I can see the rows of trees behind my childhood home where we used to play. I find that scents can trigger the best memories."

Kayleigh thought of the pots of lavender in the sunroom of her house. The scent of their bright purple flowers always reminded her of her mother. They used to dry the densely branched stalks and flowers for potpourri.

"What brings you here today?" Mrs. Rouhani asked.

"I'm not sure," Kayleigh said. "Mrs. Williams suggested I come."

"Are you not feeling well?"

"I'm not sick. I feel...off. I don't know how to explain it." Kayleigh sighed and ran her fingers through her hair. "I just feel so jumpy, like sometimes the smallest thing can startle me."

"It sounds like hyperarousal."

"No! No, it's not. I'm not aroused." Kayleigh shifted in her seat, turned bright red, and pulled on a strand of her hair. The nurse couldn't know she'd just been texting with Nate.

Mrs. Rouhani laughed a light chuckle that was almost musical. "Hyperarousal is when you are easily startled. You may feel on edge. It happens to people after traumatic events."

Kayleigh sighed, relieved they weren't talking about the *other* kind of arousal. "Exactly. I can't relax. I figured it was just stress." She gazed at the nurse's face, her creamy skin and deep brown eyes. The nurse's presence soothed Kayleigh.

"Was that why Mrs. Williams sent you in?" Mrs. Rouhani asked.

"Not exactly. I was talking to myself, and I felt like I was about to jump out of my skin."

Mrs. Rouhani cocked her head at Kayleigh and drew her brows together.

"I know that sounds bad, but I was just trying to calm myself down." She shifted on the cot and played with her hair. "Sometimes I let the world go fuzzy. That's how I'm able to escape for just a while. When I'm really stressed, I drift off and imagine I'm with my mother."

"You must really miss her," Mrs. Rouhani said. She touched Kayleigh's hand and stopped it from tugging on her hair. Mrs. Rouhani clasped the hair and smoothed it behind Kayleigh's ear. Kayleigh nodded.

"There's regular stress, and then there's the trauma you went through when you lost your mother," Mrs. Rouhani said. "I don't think this sounds like typical stress. I'd like to call Mr. Stanley. Would that be okay?"

Kayleigh nodded again and sniffed.

Mrs. Rouhani went to the phone and dialed an extension. "Arthur, would you mind coming to my office, please?"

A few moments later, Mr. Stanley arrived. He smiled at Kayleigh. "We have to stop meeting this way."

Kayleigh giggled, remembering the last time they spoke after she fainted.

"Fill me in on what's going on," he said.

Kayleigh summarized what had happened in the classroom and how she had felt in the hallway. She was truthful about what she had experienced, except for the part about thinking she was a morph.

"So you sometimes feel on edge, jumpy, and other times you feel detached or fuzzy," he summarized. "How about any nightmares? Trouble sleeping?" he asked.

Kayleigh nodded. "A few. Sometimes."

"Any flashbacks or re-experiencing the day your mother disappeared?"

Kayleigh shook her head. She remembered that day every once in a while, but it didn't pop into her head often. She wanted to tell Mr. Stanley she was more worried about turning into a swan, but she bit her tongue. That would probably be the fastest way to the loony bin.

"You went through a very difficult experience, finding your father injured and your mother gone. PTSD, or Post Traumatic Stress Disorder, can cause hyperarousal, feelings of being detached, flashbacks, avoidance, and other symptoms. Although you don't have all of those, it seems like you have more than the average amount of stress."

Kayleigh nodded. *If you only knew.*

"So I'd like to talk to your father about how best to help you, okay?" he asked.

"Sure," she said.

"Are you all right now to return to English?"

"Yeah, I'm fine."

"Right. Head on back to class, and I'll check in with you tomorrow."

Mrs. Rouhani walked her to the door. "Come again if you need to, Kayleigh."

"Okay, thanks." She pushed the door open, paused, and turned back towards Mrs. Rouhani. The nurse had already gone to Mr. Stanley. They whispered, their heads close, brows drawn.

An unease filled Kayleigh. She was already trying to deal with being a Morph. PTSD sounded like something soldiers got from war, not something regular people got. She pushed that thought out of her head, afraid she would look down and see she'd morphed into camouflage. Things were getting more complicated by the minute.

CHAPTER SIX
THE DATE

Saturday came quicker than Kayleigh would have liked. Threads of worry revolved in her mind, spinning as intricately as the never-ending Celtic knots carved into the chest containing the secrets of her family tree.

Bridget waited with Kayleigh in the family room for Daiyu's mom to arrive. Mrs. Sun had agreed to drive them to the movies, and Ben's father would pick them up later.

"You have the jitters?" Bridget asked. "It looks like you can't keep your hands steady."

"I don't think I can do this," Kayleigh said. She paced in front of the windows and watched the street. The snowplow had been by to clear the roadway, leaving mounds of gray slush on the sidewalks.

"Do what? Go to the movies or let Daiyu's mom pick us up?" Bridget asked.

"Go on a date with Nate," Kayleigh said. She pressed a hand against her stomach, which threatened to lodge itself in her throat.

"A group date," Bridget said. She grinned at Kayleigh and held up her thumb and forefinger an inch apart. "A little date."

"Whatever kind of date, I can't go. It'll be a disaster." Kayleigh plunked on the couch and let her shoes land on the floor with a thud. Nerves clouded her judgment, and despair muddied her thinking.

Bridget strolled to Kayleigh. She smoothed the skirt of her red dress underneath her and perched on the edge of the sofa. She started to say something, but paused. She frowned, looked at her skirt for several minutes, and eventually spoke in measured tones.

"I'm trying to figure out the best way to say this nicely," Bridget ran a hand over the hem of her skirt. "You're starting to get annoying."

"That's the nice version?" Kayleigh asked.

"Well, yes, it is. The other version involved calling you a coward."

"Gee, don't sugarcoat it." Kayleigh sank into the cushions, and her head dropped onto her chest.

"I get that you went through something awful and that you still think something is happening to you. But you've started whining a bunch lately."

"Okay, I get it. You don't want to hear my problems."

"It's not that I don't wanna listen. It's that I'm wondering why you don't do something. Who wants to be worried all the time?" Bridget stood and strode around the coffee table. She whirled and faced Kayleigh, her dress swinging out like a fan around her legs.

"You have no idea how great you have it here, and yet all you do is complain. Whine, whine, bullies. Whine, whine, morph. Whine, whine, Nate. Whine, whine, my mo—"

"Stop." Kayleigh said. She jumped to her feet, and her hands formed fists at her side. "What is wrong with you?"

Bridget stalked to the window. She lifted her hair off her neck, exhaled, and pressed her forehead to the glass. "Have you ever wondered why I came here?"

"To the U.S.?" Kayleigh asked.

"Why do you think I entered a cultural program thousands of miles away from home?" Bridget puffed on the glass and fogged up the window. She drew a four-leaf clover with her finger in the condensation.

"To experience our culture?"

"That's true, but that's not the entire reason." She pushed away from the window and studied her artwork. "I wasn't welcome at home."

"Not welcome?" Kayleigh frowned and studied Bridget's face.

"My father couldn't accept me for who I am, so I left." She crossed her arms over her torso.

"Bridget, I'm sorry. You never told me." Kayleigh rose and went to stand by her friend. She slipped an arm around Bridget's middle, stood on her tiptoes, and rested her head on the top of her pal's shoulder. An ache formed around Kayleigh's heart to see her closest confidant in pain and to not have known.

Bridget smiled and let her head rest on top of Kayleigh's. "My host family, at least, leaves me alone for the most part so I can do my thing."

Kayleigh saw Mrs. Sun's Volvo pull up the front drive. Daiyu saw them standing in the window and waved.

"I'll tell you the whole tale another time," Bridget said. She pulled away and retrieved her coat from the hallway.

A blast of frigid air rushed over them when Kayleigh opened the front door. She adjusted her scarf and pulled her coat up to her chin. She followed Bridget to the car, her shoulders hunched against the wind. Bridget opened the back door and motioned for Kayleigh to get in. Kayleigh slid across the backseat to sit next to Ben, and Bridget sat on her other side.

"Hi, guys," Daiyu said. She turned from the front seat and smiled.

"Hi, Daiyu," Kayleigh said. "Hi, Mrs. Sun."

"*Nǐmén hǎo*, girls. Happy Valentine's Day to you," Mrs. Sun said. Kayleigh enjoyed listening to her high melodic accent and the occasional word in Mandarin. The Suns had immigrated to the States from China the year Daiyu was born.

"Are you ready to see *Underneath These Stormy Skies*?" Daiyu asked. "It's supposed to be both romantic and heartbreaking."

"The perfect chick flick," Ben said. He grumbled something incoherent under his breath.

"What was that?" Daiyu asked.

"Nothing. Looking forward to it." He forced a smile through clenched teeth. "For reals," he said to Daiyu in particular.

She squinted at him.

"How about you?" Ben asked Kayleigh.

"I think Nate wants to see the action one, something about hackers."

"Why doesn't he have to see the chick flick?" Ben asked. His voice took on a whiny edge. Kayleigh winced, remembering how Bridget had called her a whiner.

"He asked me to see it with him. I said yes."

"Stop your bellyaching, Benjamin," Bridget said. This was the first thing she had said since they'd gotten in the car. "You don't have to do anything. I'm sure Daiyu would rather you see what you want than risk having to listen to you gripe all evening. She could go see the movie she wants without you. Isn't that right, D?"

Daiyu's eyes opened wide, and her eyebrows lifted in surprise. "Sure. Whatever," she said. Ben looked across the car at Bridget and then at Kayleigh.

Mrs. Sun glanced through the rear view mirror at Bridget. "You feel all right, Bridget?"

"I'm fine, sorry." Bridget fell silent for the rest of the ride.

Kayleigh reflected on what Bridget had said about her father, and how he couldn't accept Bridget. That would be like a knife through the heart, a pain so deep anyone would want to run halfway across the world to escape. Kayleigh wondered what would happen if she told her father about being a morph. Unless she could show him, he might not believe her, and even then, he might not accept her.

Daiyu's mother pulled up to the movie theater. "Everyone have a good time," she said.

"Thank you for the ride, Mrs. Sun," Kayleigh said.

"You're welcome, Kayleigh. *Wŏ ài nĭ*, Daiyu," Mrs. Sun said.

"I love you, too, Mom," Daiyu said.

Inside the cinema, they removed their hats and coats. Kayleigh's hands shook while she unbuttoned her jacket. She looked around for Nate while her stomach did flips.

"I'll get the popcorn," Bridget said. She walked off, her strides long and graceful in three-inch heels.

"You made it." Nate's low voice came from behind Kayleigh, and the smooth baritone sent shivers down her spine. *So these were the good kind of goose bumps Bridget was talking about.*

"It appears so." She turned and smiled at him. Nate was wearing a bright cobalt button-down shirt, which made his eyes seem as blue as cornflowers. The warm shudder only lasted a moment. She was on a date. An actual date. Panic replaced pleasure. It pressed at the back of her throat, threatening to cut off her airway, but she resisted the urge to run. She knew she should be excited, starry eyed. Instead terror gripped her similar to when the dentist took out her wisdom teeth. It wasn't rational.

"Hey, Nate, howya been?" Ben asked. He stepped past Kayleigh and slapped Nate on the upper arm. "I hear you wanna watch the cyber-attack movie."

Kayleigh snuck a look at Daiyu, who rolled her eyes. Ben could be sweet, but he clearly did not want to see the chick flick. Daiyu shook her head and shrugged.

Nate nodded. "Yeah, it's supposed to be awesome."

"And it will point out how vulnerable we are with so much information online," Ben said. "That could just be a way of telling me to get off the computer and do more homework."

Nate laughed, which reminded Kayleigh of smooth honey and warm tea. She felt the tension slip out of her limbs. This wouldn't be so bad.

"Hello, everyone, good to see you." A shrill voice rose over the laughter. Kayleigh turned to see Hannah arrive, pulling Martin by the hand. His mouth was pinched, his eyebrows pulled together. He staggered behind her, as reluctant as a puppy on a leash for the first time.

Hannah beamed at them and nudged a space between Nate and Kayleigh, so that she and Martin could stand in their circle.

"This is so great. All of us here at the movies on Valentine's Day, right?" Hannah said. She bounced twice on her toes and squeezed Martin's hand. The lace hem of her skirt fluttered with each movement, and her long chestnut hair swung across the middle of her back.

Kayleigh realized she didn't really know Hannah. She knew of her, mostly because she was friends with Emma. That immediately made Kayleigh dislike her, but she tried to reserve judgment.

"What movie are you going to see?" Kayleigh forced a smile and tried to convince herself to relax.

"*Underneath These Stormy Skies,*" Martin said. He pushed the words out through gritted teeth.

"It's supposed to be stirring and uplifting," Daiyu said.

"Or boring," Ben said.

"It's the perfect date movie," Hannah said. She leaned into Martin and sighed.

"It's a date movie?" Nate asked. He turned to Kayleigh, his blond head cocked to one side. "Do you want to see that one instead?"

Kayleigh's cheeks flushed at the word date, while Martin rolled his eyes. Daiyu put her hands on her hips and glared at Ben. Kayleigh stared at Nate but couldn't form words.

Bridget arrived from getting snacks. "Whoa, what kinda hornets' nest am I walking back into?" She held two huge tubs of buttered popcorn.

"We're discussing whether to watch the date-night movie about young lovers, or the one about hackers overthrowing the government with computers," Kayleigh explained.

"I vote for the star-crossed lovers," Hannah said. She looked up at Martin and batted her eyes.

"And I vote for cyber-attacks," Ben said.

"Why do we all have to watch the same movie?" Bridget asked.

"I thought the idea was to spend Valentine's Day together, as a *group,* remember?" Martin asked Bridget. He gestured with his head towards Hannah, who still clung to his hand.

"All right, then. Let's put it to a vote." Bridget stood tall and used a commanding tone. "All in favor of *Stormy Skies* raise your hand."

Hannah's hand shot up immediately, and she lifted onto her toes. Daiyu's hand went into the air, but she sighed when she only saw one other hand.

"So we've got two votes for the sappy romance," Bridget said. "Which means the rest of us vote for action. Cyber-attack wins." She marched off towards the theater.

Ben jumped and gave Martin a high five. Hannah's lip formed a pout, and she looked at Martin, but he shrugged his shoulders. "Majority wins."

Daiyu mumbled something about having the wrong tickets, but she followed Bridget into the section showing the action movie.

Nate held open the door for Kayleigh, and her heart quickened. His platinum hair swooped across his forehead, and the ends brushed his eyebrows. He smiled and gestured with one palm up, which reminded her of a Boy Scout helping old ladies across the street. She relaxed.

The previews had already started, and it was dark. Between flashes of light from the screen, she could see Daiyu waving at them from halfway up on the other side. Kayleigh followed the small lights at the base of the stairs and found where her friends had left them two seats at the end of the row. She sank into a velvet cushion, grateful to have a couple of hours without conversation.

The movie proved to be as expected, a typical action movie — bad guys try to take over the world — with a computer twist. Kayleigh was relieved it didn't take a whole lot of brainpower to watch, nor did it tug at her heartstrings. Crying during a movie might open up the floodgates to feelings better kept locked away.

The lights came up as the credits rolled. Kayleigh stood and stretched her legs. Relieved she had gotten through the movie, she told herself the date was almost over.

"Where should we go now?" Nate asked. He looked at Kayleigh and the group, his eyes bright. He only needed to pull out a compass, and Kayleigh could imagine him on a mountaintop, planning the next treacherous trek with serene optimism.

Kayleigh scanned her friends and wasn't sure anyone was in the mood for more Valentine's fun. Daiyu had her arms crossed and still glared at Ben, who was watching Hannah. Hannah still held Martin's hand in a vice grip, and she didn't seem to notice he shifted back and forth on his feet as if he needed to use the boys' room. Bridget stood at the other end of the row, examining her nail polish.

"Now? Aren't we done?" A pit formed in Kayleigh's stomach. Martin nodded in agreement.

"It's not even 10 pm," Nate said. "There's a cake place next door. How about we get some dessert?"

"Now, doesn't that sound romantic?" Hannah looked at Martin, which forced him to smile. Kayleigh guessed that he didn't want to be outright rude, but clearly he wasn't having a good time.

A war raged within Kayleigh. On one hand, she wanted to end the date while she was ahead. On the other hand, she liked the butterflies in her stomach when Nate smiled at her. Since she couldn't figure out how to end the date early without hurting Nate, she said, "Okay, let them eat cake."

Bridget raised one eyebrow at Kayleigh, while Hannah squealed with pleasure. Kayleigh walked down the theater stairs, feeling more like she was pushing her luck. Something terrible was bound to happen.

She recognized that the nerves cramping her stomach reflected irrational anxiety, but she couldn't soothe herself.

Her mind went to the most extreme places when her nerves took over. Illogical scenarios about what might happen in the cake shop flashed in her head. One unjustifiable scene even involved huge swans crashing through the windows and carrying Nate off as her body morphed from one grotesque form to another.

Kayleigh sighed and tried to control her breathing as they walked. The dessert shop was next door, but still required they step outside for a moment. The wintry air rushed over her cheeks, and a chill ran through her extremities. She concentrated on the goose bumps that had sprung up on her arms, a welcome distraction from the torrent of thoughts in her mind.

Kayleigh entered the bakery, and a deluge of crimson hearts overwhelmed her. Cardboard Cupids lined the walls, and streamers entwined the cases of pastries.

"Cupcakes," Hannah said. She bounced to Nate and threw her arms around his neck. "What a perfect idea for Valentine's Day."

Nate blushed and lowered his head. When he looked at Kayleigh, his sapphire eyes peeping through golden bangs, it caused a warmth to spread outward from below her belly. She felt the breath catch in her throat and smiled in return.

"Who would've thought you were so romantic, Nate?" Hannah asked. She still had her arms around his neck. She glanced at Martin, who studied the rows of different types of cupcakes on display.

Nate's eyes widened, and he looked down at Hannah. Hannah gazed at Nate, her emerald eyes accented with plum liner and dark mascara. A surge of white-hot jealousy rippled through Kayleigh.

"All right, everyone. Let's not hover in the doorway," Bridget said. She pushed Martin towards Hannah and scowled at him. Martin frowned back at Bridget, but held out his hand for Hannah. She took Martin's hand, but continued to smile at Nate as Martin pulled her into the line to order.

"Wow, look at all the types of cupcakes," Hannah said.

"Why don't you have a seat, Kayleigh, and I'll get one for you?" Nate said. "You're looking a little — "

"Thanks, I'll have a red velvet," Kayleigh said, interrupting him. Whatever he was about to say wouldn't have been flattering.

Daiyu glowered at Ben, but he looked down at his wallet. She sighed and got in line with Hannah. Kayleigh winced, for Daiyu seemed as miserable as Martin. Hannah didn't seem to notice the tension, however, and she continued to gush over the various flavors of cake.

"I'll sit with you," Bridget said.

Kayleigh found a round table in the back, and they seated themselves. The tables had been covered with red paper tablecloths and white doilies.

"I'd watch that Hannah," Bridget said. "She might have realized Martin's not her type, after all. Nate might be." She pointed to where Hannah stood next to Nate. Kayleigh was too far away to hear what she said, but Hannah's bright smile and her hand on Nate's arm spoke volumes.

"Great, something else to worry about," Kayleigh said. She fiddled with the edge of a paper napkin, twisting it into a point.

"Didn't we already have this conversation?" Bridget asked. Kayleigh didn't miss the bitter sarcasm that dripped from the Irish girl's words.

The air, sweet with the scent of sugar and vanilla, clogged Kayleigh's throat. A local radio station played the biggest ballads from the last century, which expressed love, trust, betrayal, and heartache. Whitney Houston crooned, "I will always love you," and a queasy feeling lurched in Kayleigh's stomach.

She watched Nate order their cupcakes and smile at something Hannah said, while she pointed at a sugary confection in the glass case. As the server brought out the treat, decorated in pink frosting with multicolored sprinkles, Hannah grabbed Nate's arm, giggled, and jumped up on her toes.

Kayleigh groaned. The whole sickly sweet scene made her want to throw up. Without context, it was almost like Nate was on a date with Hannah. Kayleigh took a breath as another gush of stomach acid and jealousy climbed up her throat.

Kayleigh looked up at the ceiling where silver balloons with scalloped edges floated peacefully. She knew Bridget wanted her to be more assertive, but she'd rather drift away like a helium balloon.

A warm tingle spread over her skin, and a sense of calm settled upon her. Her mind floated above the people, where the glint of silver balloons sparkled off the recessed lighting. Her skin shifted to match the picture in her head, becoming shiny and light. Her bottom lifted off the chair, and her feet skimmed the floor. Round. Warm. Weightless.

"What are you doing?" Bridget hissed under her breath. "People will notice." She stabbed Kayleigh in the leg with a metal fork from the place setting.

"Ouch!" The pain broke Kayleigh's concentration, and the air whooshed out of her body at the puncture wounds with a soft *whee*. Her body sank back into the chair, and her arms fell limp at her sides.

The warm tingle of morphing subsided, replaced with an icy fear. It would have been a relief to simply float away. Tears welled in her eyes. She couldn't let her mind drift off for fear of physically becoming whatever she imagined, and yet she longed to let her mind fade away to anywhere else to escape this awkward date. It should have been great that her dream guy had asked her out on Valentine's Day, but she couldn't relax enough to enjoy herself. Nate even seemed to be flirting more with Hannah. Nowhere to hide, not even in her own mind. This date couldn't get worse.

She scanned the exits, wondering if she could leave and call her father to pick her up before she morphed into a car and drove herself home.

As she surveyed the front doors to calculate the likelihood of being able to bolt, both sides opened with a whoosh of cold air, and Emma stepped through like a royal princess entering her court.

Correction, the date just got worse.

Hannah let out a high-pitched squeal as she caught sight of Emma.

Just my luck. The air became very thin and Kayleigh opened her mouth, trying to get more oxygen. A knot formed in Kayleigh's chest, and she placed her fingers against her breastbone, trying to rub out an ache that burned like a muscle cramp.

"Stay cool, Kayleigh," Bridget said. "And stay *here.*" She slid a hand over Kayleigh's arm and pressed on her wrist, stopping her from floating off again.

"Hannah, imagine running into you here," Emma said. They leaned close and air-kissed each other. *Muah Muah.*

When Emma pulled back and sent a smirk in Kayleigh's direction, Kayleigh realized that it was not a coincidence that Emma had showed up. Hannah must have texted her on the walk from the theater.

"So, Hannah, I see you're here with Nate, tonight," Emma said loudly, looking over again at Kayleigh. Hannah had the decency to pull her arm quickly away from Nate, sink her head into her shoulders with guilt, and step closer to Martin.

"I'm here with Martin," she said. Her cheeks became as ruby as a ceramic heart on the counter, and she brushed a lock of hair behind her ear. She traced the hole of a ruffle on her dress and glanced between the two boys.

"Isn't that nice," Emma said. She practically purred and leaned towards Martin. She ran her fingernails over his arm. "Aren't you lucky to be here with such a pretty girl. I didn't think Hannah was your . . . type."

Martin flinched and pulled back from Emma, who snickered. Clearly she was enjoying making everyone uncomfortable.

"And Daiyu," Emma said. "It looks like you finally caught your prince." Daiyu's eyes widened. Emma hadn't ever spoken to her directly. Emma sauntered to her, gave her a light nudge with her elbow, and gestured at Ben. "And what a frog prince he is."

The server finished a transaction and handed Nate a tray with cupcakes and hot chocolate. Nate stood motionless and directed his gaze at Emma's handbag, rather than her eyes.

"And Nate," Emma said. "Who'd you bring tonight?" Her eyes narrowed, and she sought Nate's eye contact, as menacing as Medusa seeking victims to turn to stone.

"I'm here with Kayleigh." His voice cracked on Kayleigh's name, and he coughed to clear his throat. He shifted away from Emma and took several steps towards the table.

"Kayleigh's here?" The exaggerated singsong tone of her voice confirmed that Emma had arrived expecting to crash Kayleigh's date. "Why don't I join all of you?"

Hannah studied Emma for a moment and hesitated. "Sure, why not?" Her voice wavered.

As Hannah turned and walked towards the table, Kayleigh wondered if Hannah knew Emma had tricked her. Kayleigh had always thought of Hannah as Emma's accomplice, two peas in a pod. Even their names semi-rhymed. Hannah certainly always seemed to stand by Emma whenever she taunted Kayleigh. Maybe she'd misread Hannah as being guilty by association.

As Emma and the group approached, Bridget slid to the edge of her chair, and the hand on Kayleigh's arm squeezed tighter. Kayleigh had the distinct feeling they should prepare for battle.

"Hello, Kayleigh. I never thought I'd run into you out on Valentine's Day." Emma fired the first shot.

"Clearly," Kayleigh said. She worked to control her breathing.

Kayleigh's friends all took seats around the table like pieces on a chessboard. Nate sat next to Kayleigh and gave her the red velvet cupcake. Emma stood behind the empty seat next to Bridget.

"And out with Nate?" Emma asked. "Who would have thought a ten like Nate would settle for a two like you?" She emphasized the last syllable with a sneer that lifted the top of her lip towards her nose.

Kayleigh closed her eyes, and her skin shuddered. She struggled to clear her mind of any image that would result in morphing.

"Really, Nate," Emma said. "I'd have thought you'd want a more assertive woman, not a scaredy-girl."

"Emma, cut it out," Nate said. His low voice rumbled across the table.

Kayleigh stood and opened her mouth. Now was the chance to say something profound, something that would shut Emma up once and for all. She took a deep breath and turned towards Emma.

"Yes?" Emma asked. She placed one hand on her hip and raised her eyebrows.

She opened her mouth to speak, prepared to throw down a world of hurt. Instead, she listened to instinct and ran.

"Excuse me," Kayleigh said. The urge to run was too strong. She slid past the table and towards the restroom, before everyone saw the tears about to slide down her face.

She heard Emma laughing behind her, which stopped as soon as Bridget asked, "So where's your date, Em?"

Kayleigh shut herself in a stall and sat on the lid of the toilet seat. She slumped against the side, her forehead pressed against the cool metal. Plump tears rolled over the edges of her eyes and splashed onto her sweater.

She had done nothing to Emma. Ever. Not an unkind word, nor a look, nothing. And yet Emma kept coming after her.

The door to the bathroom opened, the bottom edge scraping along the tiled floor. Footsteps followed.

"Kayleigh?" Daiyu's soft voice sailed over the partition.

"Here," Kayleigh said.

"Are you okay?"

"It seems many people have been asking me that lately, and I don't know how to answer."

"Other than to say Emma's a *biotch*," Daiyu said.

"Most definitely."

Kayleigh blew her nose with toilet paper, and a *honk* echoed against the tile. Several more tears wet the tissue, and the tension bottled up in her rib cage dissipated. She leaned over and unlocked the stall door. It slowly swung inward, and she caught it with her foot. Daiyu stood on the other side, wringing her hands. A wry smile dimpled one cheek.

She remembered the first time she had seen Daiyu. Her first memory. They were three years old, and Kayleigh hadn't seen a Chinese child before. To Kayleigh, Daiyu looked exactly like a porcelain doll that her mother had given her, complete with ebony hair and a heavy fringe of bangs. Daiyu even had locks of hair twisted into buns, one on each side of her head above her ears.

Now Daiyu's hair was cut into a bob, but the same narrow eyes peered from under a curtain of black. She smiled at Kayleigh, cocked her head to one side, and shrugged her shoulders.

"So why let Emma get to you?" Daiyu asked. "Nate doesn't look like he enjoys Hannah's attention so much."

"It's not that." Kayleigh sighed and pressed a tissue to her eyes. "I mean, it's not fun to watch a girl flirt with the guy you like, and it's certainly not my idea of a good time to be called names in front of my friends, but I have other stuff to worry about that's…bigger."

"Grades?" Daiyu guessed.

"No, not grades. Mine aren't very good, so I should worry about them, but no," Kayleigh said. She crossed to the mirror and saw her face, streaked with tears. "Ugh. I have to stop looking in the mirror when I'm like this."

Kayleigh ran some tepid water and splashed her face, thankful she hadn't let Bridget put any makeup on her tonight. She pulled out a comb from her pocket and tried to detangle her auburn waves but decided it was easier to gather her hair into a loose ponytail at the nape of her neck.

"Is it your mom?" Daiyu asked.

"Partially. I miss her. And it's not that my dad is a horrible parent, but he's not my mom."

"Your mom was always laughing. When I visited your house, I remember being surprised that adults could be so fun. My parents certainly weren't…aren't."

"My dad doesn't laugh so much anymore," Kayleigh said. "I don't help by moping around the house. And certainly not by keeping secrets, but I'm dealing with stuff that he couldn't understand."

"What do you mean, secrets? What else is going on?"

Beep beep. Kayleigh's phone signaled the arrival of a text.

Nate: u ok?

Kayleigh: not feeling well.

Nate: Emma left.

"It's Nate," Kayleigh said. "He says Emma left."

"So let's go back out," Daiyu said.

Beep beep.

Nate: need anything?

Kayleigh: no, thanks. will call my dad to pick me up. have fun with others. sorry.

Nate: no apology needed. Happy Valentine's Day.

Kayleigh: thanks. Happy Valentine's Day to you, too.

"Daiyu, thanks for coming in to talk, but I really just need to go home." Kayleigh dialed her father.

Daiyu's face fell, but she nodded. "Okay, I'll tell the others you're sick."

Kayleigh watched her leave, and guilt clawed at the inside of her chest. She and Daiyu had been friends for twelve years, but when Kayleigh found out she was a morph, she had called Bridget. Perhaps she had confided in Bridget because of the Irish legend. But maybe, if she was honest, it was because she sensed that Bridget also kept secrets.

CHAPTER SEVEN

FRIENDS

S everal weeks had flown by since Valentine's Day. Soon it would be spring break, although gray slush still dampened the ground. The temperature had dropped below freezing for several days, transforming the pavement into a skating rink of black ice.

Kayleigh sat at the kitchen table, stirring a cup of chamomile and absently petting the cat, which folded its paws next to her on the bench and purred. Steam rose and curled into question marks. She absently caressed the key hanging off her necklace, once again a pendant. It had no more secrets to unlock, its job done.

Nate had texted her several times, but Kayleigh still couldn't bring herself to accept another date. The embarrassment of that night clung to her body like an ugly holiday sweater in gaudy colors. Her cheeks flushed and her palms sweated under its oppressive weight. She wished she could escape the discomfort, but she couldn't trust herself not to morph into a balloon and sail away merely by imagining it.

And which was worse—turning into a floating object or standing in front of Emma like a defenseless lamb waiting to be slaughtered?

Her father walked into the kitchen and poured more hot water into his mug. He opened the box of teas and sifted through the thin envelopes. "How's your wild chamomile?"

"It's supposed to be relaxing, but I don't think I like tea very much."

Her father laughed, a quiet chuckle that broke the hush of the morning. She looked up with surprise, not remembering the last time he had laughed.

"What's so funny?"

"Just now you sounded so much like your mother." He sat across from her and unwrapped a black chai. "She used to hate tea. Always complained about how the Brits drank so much flavored water. Then, she found lavender tea. Suddenly it was lavender flavored Earl Grey, lavender plants, lavender perfume..." His voice trailed off and melancholy darkened his face like the sun disappearing over the horizon at sunset.

"Lavender reminds me of Mom," Kayleigh said.

"Me, too." He dropped his bag into the mug and dunked it several times. "I'm sorry she's not here to help you go through whatever it is that's bothering you right now."

"What do you mean?"

"I've noticed you're different lately. Since school started back after break, you've been quieter."

"I've been studying more."

"That's not what I mean. You seem lost in thought."

Just lost, Dad. Kayleigh took a sip of her chamomile, which reminded her of fresh apples. She enjoyed the closeness that she usually had with her father, but she hesitated over which details of recent events to share with him.

"You've been especially gloomy since Valentine's Day," he said.

"Cuz that night was just epic." Her voice reeked of sarcasm, and she resented Fate for handing her such circumstances.

"I thought you liked Nate."

Kayleigh took a deep breath and decided to tell her father part of what had happened on Valentine's Day. "I do like Nate, but I hate Emma. And I'm worried that Nate likes Hannah."

"Nate likes Emma or Hannah?"

"Hannah."

"So who's Emma?" Her father's brows drew together with confusion, and he stopped sipping.

"Emma Vanderweele is a spoiled brat who thinks she can stomp on anyone she wants." Rage rushed through Kayleigh, raw like an open wound.

"Vanderweele. That's not a common last name. Her father's in IT?"

Kayleigh nodded. Relief soothed the tension in her muscles, and she was grateful she could talk to her father, unlike Bridget.

"Her older brother's in my intro-level history class," her father said. "I think his father wanted him to go into the computer business, but my impression is he likes the humanities."

"Good for him. But his little sister's a bi—"

"Kayleigh!" Her father cut her off before she could swear in his presence. He used to joke that her mother had a mouth that belonged on a sailor, but Kayleigh knew he wouldn't tolerate her using such words.

"I'm sorry. I just can't stand her. She calls me names, both in public, and on her Me3 page."

"If she's a bully, then there are actions you can take," her father said.

"I know, but none of the options seem great. Daiyu thinks I should go to the administration. Bridget thinks I should fight her back, physically, I think. Natalie thinks I should hack

Emma's page—which we would never do, by the way." She glanced nervously at her father and back at her tea.

"New York has anti-bullying laws, as do many states nowadays. Schools are obligated to address the harassment and help the victim."

"Ugh, Dad. Words like 'harassment' and 'victim' are precisely why I just want it to go away." She grabbed the key around her neck and tugged on it, pulling her neck down until her chin rested on her hands.

"Wait—let me see that." Her father reached over to open her hands. "Is that a key?"

Something in his urgent tone made the hairs on the back of her neck stand up. He looked so intently at the key it startled her. She lifted her head, and the key slipped past her hands and landed with a clatter on the wooden table. As she pulled back, it scraped along the wood until it swung to rest on her cardigan.

"That was your mother's."

"I know. It was left for me." Goosebumps sprang up on her arms, and a nervous chill slid over her back.

"How did you get it?" He pushed back from the table and stood, brows furrowed, eyes narrowed. His hands dropped, rigid, to his sides. Kayleigh couldn't tell if he was angry or concerned. Usually she read her father easily.

"Mrs. O'Neill says the postman dropped it off," Kayleigh said. Alarmed at his demeanor, she wasn't sure if she should tell him their neighbor may or may not have lied about that fact.

"Your mother wore that necklace," he repeated.

"I figured she did," Kayleigh said.

"She wore that necklace every day. She said the swan reminded her of Ireland."

"There's a legend," Kayleigh said, connecting the dots.

"The Children of Lir, I know." His voice became louder and more strident.

"Dad, why are you so upset? I miss Mom, too, but you seem angry."

"Your mother wore that necklace every day, Kayleigh. Every. Day. She never took it off. She had to have been wearing it the day she—"

He abruptly stopped, and a sob escaped his lips. He raised a fist to his mouth and drew in a sharp breath. Kayleigh's stomach plummeted to the floor.

"What does that mean?" Kayleigh asked. "That she sent it here?"

"Or someone took it off her bo—"

"No!" Now it was Kayleigh's turn to cut him off. "I will not let you finish that sentence." She stood and stumbled over the wooden bench. Guilt flooded through her that she'd been more focused on Nate than on finding her mother. "Mom is still alive, and I will find her."

Kayleigh ran out of the kitchen and through the family room. She grabbed her coat and paused in the hallway by the front door. Her father, still in the kitchen, began to sob, a raw, guttural sound muffled by the walls in between them.

Her father had always been stoic, his eyes barely watering at his own father's funeral. An image of her father, his face purple and caked with blood, lying on the floor of his study, flashed into her mind. The truth of her father's physical vulnerability had smacked her in the face two years ago. The anguish originating from the kitchen was much worse.

She didn't know what could possibly help her father at this moment, and the urge to flee overwhelmed her. She needed answers, something to show him there was still hope of finding her mother. Silly crushes and Irish myths had distracted her from the more important task of finding her mother. The thought of getting clarity propelled her out the door and down the sidewalk to Mrs. O'Neill's house.

Her neighbor's house sat on a wooded lot with a long front path bordered by Japanese maples. During the winter, the branches were absent of wine-colored foliage, but the ice coating the graceful arms of the trees accented their round shape. In the spring, Mrs. O'Neill spent hours outside pruning the Lace Leaf into domes under which rabbits, foxes, and chipmunks would find shelter.

Kayleigh paused halfway up the front walk and looked into one of the windows lining the other side of the path. A woman sat in the front room, curled up in an oversized chair, reading a novel. She had amber tresses that fell around her face and light skin. She might have been about the same age as Kayleigh's mom, so she guessed this was Mrs. O'Neill's daughter.

She continued to the front door and rang the bell. She could see the foyer through glass panes on either side of the door. Footsteps approached.

Mrs. O'Neill passed the window in a blur of white hair, wrinkled skin, and a Mexican-themed caftan of cerulean blue, fuchsia, and tangerine with long tassels dangling off the edges. The door swung open.

"Kayleigh, dear, what a surprise," Mrs. O'Neill said. Her smile deepened the lines around her mouth, and her eyes twinkled from her weathered face.

"I'm sorry to show up unannounced," Kayleigh said. She hesitated on the threshold, shifting her feet as if a giant spotlight highlighted her awkward stance. Since her neighbor had company, it would probably be better to come back at another time.

"Lass, you don't need any reason to pop over." She pulled the door wider and motioned for Kayleigh to come in.

"Was that your daughter?" Kayleigh asked.

"I don't have—oh, you mean the woman that was here. She went to lie down for a while," Mrs. O'Neill said. She chuckled and glanced towards the windows in the front room. "Please, let's sit in the parlor."

They walked back into the sitting room, which was decorated in shades of green and blue. A sage glow shone from the walls, and its color echoed throughout the patterns on the furniture. Pillows in soft blues edged with burnt sienna piping accented each chair, inviting the potential occupant to rest and relax.

"Make yourself at home, and I'll get us some lavender Earl Grey," Mrs. O'Neill said. Kayleigh's ears perked up with the word lavender, wondering if it was a common tea, or if that was her first clue.

Mrs. O'Neill padded off on her bare feet, the dark wood floors creaking under her weight. When she disappeared into the kitchen, Kayleigh tiptoed to the edge of the room and peered around the corner. She could see the edge of the woman's shawl by a kitchen cabinet and hear the clinking of what she assumed must be teacups and saucers. Satisfied that Mrs. O'Neill was busy fixing the tea, Kayleigh hurried back to the room and began to look around.

There had to be some clues, anything that would tell her how Mrs. O'Neill was connected to all of this. If the postman didn't actually leave the necklace for Kayleigh, then she wanted to find out why Mrs. O'Neill had it and why she had lied. And more importantly, how did she get it? If what Kayleigh's father said was true, and her mother was wearing the necklace the day she disappeared, then Kayleigh had to know how it came off: willingly or by force.

She examined the room and noticed a small bookshelf. She bent down and scanned the titles. *Ulysses, Gulliver's Travels,*

The Picture of Dorian Gray. Nothing related to an Irish myth about stepmothers and swans.

She rose and crossed to a cabinet with glass doors. The blood pumped through her veins, and the roar of her heart sounded like the engine of a 747 in her ears. She had no desire to get caught snooping around in her neighbor's house, but her need to have answers outweighed her scruples.

A *plunk* resonated from the corner of the room, startling Kayleigh. She jumped and scanned the entrance. With a hand behind her ear, she listened for any sign that Mrs. O'Neill was on her way back. Nothing. It must have an icicle falling off the roof and hitting the sidewalk. She willed her heart to slow. *Calm down.*

She took a deep breath and peered into the cabinet, teetering on her toes. There were several blown-glass figurines of horses and flowers, reflecting the afternoon light streaming in from the windows. Serving as miniature prisms, the animals cast brilliant rainbows in all directions. Kayleigh caught sight of a swan. The ridges of its wings and the graceful curve of its neck demonstrated the skills of the glass blower who had created it. She thought it looked identical to the one her mother used to have, although glass swans were probably pretty common. A memory flashed of her feet stepping over a broken swan in the plundered family room almost three years ago.

Lavender tea. Glass swans.

She wasn't sure exactly what she was looking for, but she didn't find it among the ceramic boxes, dolls, and other knick-knacks. She sighed and dropped back on her feet.

She took a few steps to the right and studied a large painting framed in heavily gilded wood above the sofa. Colored oil paints gleamed in the muted lighting—rolling green hills, azure skies, gray mountains. A stone cottage stood in the corner, a thatched roof spilling over one side.

Wildflowers grew in clumps on the front lawn, nothing but dollops of paint in bright colors.

"That's a painting of our family home in Ireland," Mrs. O'Neill said. Kayleigh spooked and yelped—a hand flew to her chest. She quickly smiled, trying to hide the guilt she thought must be written all over her face.

On the wooden coffee table in front of the sofa, Mrs. O'Neill placed a large tray laden with two teacups and saucers, a plate of cookies, and a pot, covered with a quilted tea cozy. She sat in a matching armchair and pulled the cover off the teapot. Steam rose in swirls and curls, and the scent of lavender teased Kayleigh's nose. The image of her mother pinching herbs off the plants in the sunroom flooded her mind.

Mrs. O'Neill gazed up at the painting, and a small smile touched the corner of her mouth. "I remember when my grandmother Minnie hauled her easel, tubes of paint, and a huge canvas outside one day."

She poured tea into the cups and gestured to the sugar. Kayleigh nodded, took a seat on the sofa, and watched her neighbor drop a sugar cube into the cup with a small splash.

"Nanna sat on the other side of the clearing," Mrs. O'Neill continued and motioned for Kayleigh to sit. "Balancing on a stool the entire day, brushing away at the canvas with swirls of thick color—cadmium yellow, venetian red, raw umber."

A wistful look stole over the elderly woman's face. She smiled again and looked off into the distance. "I remember Órla and I tried to sneak around to the other side of the canvas, to see what she was painting, but we giggled too much to be stealthy. She told us to shoo and leave her to her hobby."

Mrs. O'Neill chuckled and took a sip of tea. "Nanna came back at the end of the day with that painting." Now she smiled broadly at her grandmother's artwork, her head tipped back with pride.

"Órla?" Kayleigh asked. Her cup paused midway to her lips when she recognized her mother's name.

"Your mum, of course," Mrs. O'Neill said.

"You knew my mother back in Ireland?" Kayleigh put down her cup—it clattered against the saucer—and stared at the woman as if she were seeing her for the first time.

"We used to have adventures every day, your mum and I," Mrs. O'Neill said. "We would run in the tall grass, collect wildflowers, and imagine we were fairy princesses awaiting rescue from knights on white horses."

"So you were...friends?" Kayleigh fought against the barrage of emotions that overwhelmed her—confusion, anger, fear.

"Of course, but Órla is also my cousin. Or first cousin, once removed. Something like that. My grandmother Minnie and your great-grandmother Frances were sisters."

"But I've known you for well over two years, and you never said anything." Kayleigh tried to pick up her tea, but her hands shook. She circled the outside of the cup with her other hand, the china warm and smooth. She inhaled the scent of lavender and tried to comprehend what she was hearing. A link to her mother had lived next to her for two years.

"I had to stay hidden if I didn't want to be hauled off like your mum. But I had to be close to you." She shifted forward on the cushion and took Kayleigh's cup. She set it down and took Kayleigh's hands in her own—thin, wrinkled, callused. Her blue eyes roamed over Kayleigh's face and lit up. "You look so much like her, you know," she said.

Kayleigh opened her mouth, but too many questions threatened to come tumbling forward, so she clasped it shut again. She looked down at the hands that clasped her own.

Age spots dotted the skin, and the knuckles tilted inward with arthritis. Kayleigh felt calluses scrape her skin as the woman moved her thumbs back and forth in a soothing gesture. Kayleigh would not be calmed, however.

She leapt up and jostled the tray on the coffee table. A splash of liquid spilled out of the spout and dampened the shortbread. She glared at Mrs. O'Neill, the questions tumbling forward.

"Where's my mother?" As soon as the words left her lips, her anger cooled and grief surfaced. Her eyes widened and filled with tears. "Where is she?"

Mrs. O'Neill exhaled slowly and pulled on the sleeves of her caftan. She studied a woven tassel for a moment and then looked solemnly at Kayleigh. "I wish I knew."

"How did you get the necklace? I know the postman didn't leave it for me."

"A man came to the café outside my apartment in Dublin one day. I was sitting, having tea and toast. Without preamble, he said he'd seen Órla and that it was important I get something to you." She shook her head and turned her hands over, palms up, in a gesture of awe. "Before I could ask too many questions, he'd pushed the necklace into my palm and disappeared into the crowd."

She dropped her chin and studied her open hand. Kayleigh imagined the key nestled in her palm, the chain dangling off the edge of her fingers.

"The next day a friend from the University of Syracuse messaged me that your mother had disappeared. I got on the next flight out of Ireland."

"My mother didn't just disappear," Kayleigh said. "Someone took her. And hurt my father—broke his arm and bloodied his face. He was devastated." Kayleigh began to pace, her tennis shoes clomping across the hard wood. She stopped and pivoted towards Mrs. O'Neill. "Who took her?"

"I don't know. Your father waited for a note, some request for ransom, but all he got was silence. I hadn't seen Órla for several years, so I didn't know who she might have gotten mixed up with." She folded her arms across her chest and rubbed her biceps as if to ward off a chill. "I'm sorry."

Kayleigh's head spun, and she massaged her temples with the tips of her fingers. "But she's alive."

"I believe so," Mrs. O'Neill said.

"But do we have any proof?" Kayleigh asked.

"I never spoke with her directly." Mrs. O'Neill sank down into a pillow, and her shoulders slumped.

Frustration boiled over in Kayleigh. "Then, I don't really know more about where my mother is than I did a half an hour ago. Other than some stranger in Ireland gave you her necklace. That's crap."

Kayleigh's body grew hot with fury. Every inch of her skin felt like it had caught fire, and a shimmer raced over her flesh like a flame along a trail of gunpowder. Mrs. O'Neill's eyes grew as big as saucers, and Kayleigh realized her body must have primed itself to morph. Fear doused the rage like a bucket of cold water on a campfire.

"I'm sorry. I need to go," Kayleigh stammered. Panic pushed down on her, and she ran from the room. She tore around the corner to the door and tugged on the heavy oak and glass. A rush of crisp air slapped Kayleigh in the face as she fled.

Hot tears dampened her cheeks as she rushed home. She didn't stop running until she entered her bedroom. She flung herself on the bed and let the grief swallow her into its watery grave.

Daiyu and Kayleigh sat in the library after school, attempting to study for biology. Daiyu pored over a colored diagram of a frog in preparation for their upcoming dissection lab. Kayleigh sat with her head propped on one hand, staring out a small window onto the back athletic field.

Snow still covered the bleachers, and wind whipped the flags mounted on the side of the announcer's box—the United States, the State of New York, and Onondaga High School.

She couldn't get images of Ireland out of her head, imagining her mother and Mrs. O'Neill playing in the front yard of a stone cottage lined with wildflowers.

"Hey, are you paying attention?" Daiyu asked.

"Maybe." Kayleigh looked at Daiyu, who held her head inches from the book, as if she had discovered the secret to the universe. Kayleigh recognized that look of intense concentration.

She had seen such focus the first time she had watched Daiyu practice the Chinese ribbon dance. She was maybe eight at the time, and she danced with a twelve-foot satin ribbon, exerting great effort to keep the streamer from touching the floor. One side fuchsia, the other side amethyst, it glimmered and fluttered around Daiyu's slim frame. The lower half of her body had stepped, pranced, and turned as smoothly as a ballerina, while her hands and arms swished and gyrated to keep the ribbon twirling and fluttering above her.

Kayleigh felt as pressured as the Chinese dancer, worried that if she stopped moving and thinking for one second, the cords of unease in her mind would come snaking down to entangle her.

"Listen to this, Kayleigh," Daiyu said. "In certain circumstances, when the population does not have sufficient females for procreation, frogs have been known to change their sex from male to female," Daiyu said. She read from a large animal behavior textbook.

"What?" Kayleigh sat up and forced herself to concentrate on Daiyu.

"Reed frogs," Daiyu said. "From Africa. They have been known to change sex."

"Fascinating. As long as those aren't the ones we're dissecting."

"What's fascinating?" Bridget asked. She and Natalie took seats at their table. Natalie pulled out her biology textbook.

"Frogs," Daiyu said.

"Frog princes?" Bridget asked. "We're not talking about Ben again are we?" She smirked at Daiyu and gave her a *wink*.

"Ha ha. No." Daiyu scowled at Bridget. "Just frogs." She held up her book so Bridget could see the photo of a bright African frog.

"Wonderful. What makes these so special?" Bridget said.

"They can change sex," Natalie said. She pulled out her laptop and typed. "I read it last night."

"Change sex?" Bridget asked. She took the book from Daiyu, and her eyes narrowed as she read the information box. "Too bad humans can't do so as easily."

"The psychology teacher says that's called penis envy," Natalie said. She didn't take her fingers off the laptop but glanced at Bridget and grinned.

"Funny, *Freud*," Bridget said. She flipped her hair over her shoulder, smoothed the collar of her dress, and examined her nails. "I'm just saying, if everybody could change their sex like the reed frog, maybe some people would surprise you."

"Isn't there a trans girl in twelfth grade?" Daiyu asked. "Changed his—I mean her—name from Brian to Brianna?"

"Exactly." Bridget nodded and smiled, her eyebrows raised with excitement. "She's realizing her true self."

"Uh-oh, Kayleigh," Natalie said. "Check this out." She turned her computer around to show Emma's Me3 page.

Emma had posted two pictures next to each other. The first showed Kayleigh, in her gym shorts and sweaty T-shirt. Her hair frizzed out on all sides, and her mouth gaped open like a fish, braces glinting in the sunlight.

The other picture showed Hannah with a brilliant smile, cheering at a basketball game. Her hair was pulled back in a high ponytail, adorned with ribbons, and her sleek cheer costume hugged her body, the mini skirt showing off her long tanned legs.

The caption underneath read:

P: Congrats to Nate on his upgrade. Goodbye, troll. Hello, hottie!

Kayleigh groaned when she saw the picture of herself. It had to be from last spring, the last time they'd had a track and field unit, and when she still had braces. "What does she do? Go around taking bad pictures of people and then wait for the worst time to post them?" She slumped in her chair and pulled her notebook over her face.

"Kayleigh, what does it mean Nate's upgraded to Hannah?" Daiyu asked.

"That's last week's basketball game," Natalie said. "Look."

Kayleigh sat up and followed Natalie's finger to the picture of Hannah. In the background, sitting on the first row of bleachers, was Nate, smiling directly at Hannah.

"So he's watching a basketball game," Kayleigh said. "Big deal."

"When was the last time you spoke with him?" Bridget asked.

Kayleigh blushed and ducked her head. "Valentine's Day?" She retreated back under her notebook.

"That was a month ago," Bridget said. "Did you consider he'd lose interest if you didn't answer his texts?"

"I've just had a lot on my mind." She glowered at Bridget, who waved a hand at her and made raspberry noises.

"Yeah, Kayleigh, even I know that," Daiyu said.

"What do you want to do about the picture, Kayleigh?" Natalie said. Her eyes lit up, and she cracked her knuckles.

"Don't hack her page again," Kayleigh said. She groaned. "Last time that led to Nonys and me fainting."

"Okay, let's try a different tactic," Natalie said.

Kayleigh watched as Natalie ran a search for photos of Emma. She picked an unflattering one someone had captured of Emma eating a sandwich, and she opened a program to edit it. For the next twenty minutes, Kayleigh and her friends were quiet as Natalie worked, adding to Emma's form and putting the photo through filters.

"Here you go, *Miss Thing*," Natalie said to the depiction. Her fingers swiped over the click pad as she altered the image. "Here are your improvements—a double chin, some acne, a strategically placed stain, and flabby thighs."

She turned the computer around and showed a different looking Emma. "Jeez, Natalie," Bridget said. "Remind me to never piss you off."

"I was going to give her an extra big rear end," Natalie said, "but those are actually in fashion, and I wouldn't want her to accidentally become an Internet sensation." She giggled and smiled at her handiwork.

"I don't know if anyone will actually believe this photo," Daiyu said. "Emma never leaves the house without looking perfect."

"We don't need them to believe it," Bridget said. "Just to laugh at her a little bit. An eye for an eye."

"But that assumes everyone is laughing at me over the picture Emma posted," Kayleigh said. "Maybe they don't think cyber-bullying is funny anymore."

The other girls snorted in unison, and Kayleigh knew that she was being idealistic. "In a magical land far away where everyone suddenly grew up and decided to be nice to one another." Her voice sank and she slumped into the chair.

"Some people don't recognize Emma as a cyber-bully, Kayleigh," Natalie said. "I'm sure plenty just think she's funny. Several probably think she's cool, wielding so-called power and reigning over the 9th grade." She made grand gestures to imitate a queen holding court.

"Yeah, but I don't want to stoop to her level," Kayleigh said. "Although I appreciate you wanting to defend me." Kayleigh leaned over Natalie's computer and hit *delete*.

"Friends have your back, Kayleigh," Natalie said.

Friends. Kayleigh thought of her mother and Mrs. O'Neill sneaking around together, trying to get a glimpse of their grandmother's painting.

Wait – how could they have been friends if Mrs. O'Neill's like 80 years old?

Kayleigh jumped up and knocked the book over. "Friends…sorry…but I remembered I forgot…the thing." She rushed out of the library.

The free town bus that circled between the school, Main Street, and the residential area dropped her off at the edge of her street. She jogged along the sidewalk, avoiding mounds of snow left by the plows. Her blood pumped through her body like molten lava, its warmth tinged with equal parts excitement and fear.

Her foot skated out from under her as she arrived at Mrs. O'Neill's gate, and she grabbed onto the wood planks to keep from wiping out on the ice. She hauled herself upright and pushed the gate open.

"Mrs. O'Neill," Kayleigh yelled. Her throat felt raw, and she panted as if she'd run a marathon rather than merely up the street. She pushed the doorbell repeatedly, its high cadence in stark contrast to the dull thud made from pounding on the door with her other hand. Sweat dampened her forehead and slicked her palms.

The door swung open, and Kayleigh jumped back. "Dearie, what is it?" Mrs. O'Neill asked. She motioned for Kayleigh to enter.

"How were you friends with my mother?" Kayleigh asked. The words came out in short bursts as she struggled to catch her breath.

"What do you mean?" Mrs. O'Neill frowned, and her brows drew together, which made her eyes disappear under a fold of leathery skin.

"If my mother is forty and you're...older, you wouldn't have been friends when you were both little." Kayleigh opened her jacket and pulled off her hat, suddenly dripping like a snowman in July. Her hair stood on end, charged with static electricity, waiting to deliver a shock.

Mrs. O'Neill stared at Kayleigh for a moment, smiled, and walked towards the sitting room. "Come in, dearie. Sit with me, and I'll explain."

"Tell me now."

"I was...*am* friends with your mother," Mrs. O'Neill said. "And we are cousins of the same age, actually." She walked to the nearest chair, but before sitting she turned to Kayleigh, who remained frozen in the foyer.

"How is that possible?" The question came out as a whisper, her voice hoarse.

"I'd have thought it'd be obvious," Mrs. O'Neill said. "I'm a morph."

CHAPTER EIGHT

ANNE

"What?" Kayleigh asked. An icy fear swept over her, and she took a step towards the door. In all of her pondering about being a morph, she had never considered she might meet another.

"Yes, dearie, I am a morph," Mrs. O'Neill said. She drew the curtains across the windows and turned on a pair of lamps fashioned from ceramic pots. As she clicked the last lamp on, she tilted her head back, shook her hair, and her whole body blurred, like the colors on a Monet. Her tresses, once long and white, snapped up to thick tawny curls that bounced around her shoulders. As her hair took on color, her skin lost its leathered appearance—lines and age spots smoothed and lightened. Chin and cheeks became taunt, revealing a delicate bone structure. Once curved with age, her spine straightened and pulled her shoulders back and her breasts higher in place.

Kayleigh gasped and backed into the wall. She covered her mouth to stifle her shock of seeing someone morph before her eyes.

In three seconds, it was over. The basic outline of a woman remained, but the details of her form had changed. Kayleigh was no longer looking at an elderly woman but a much younger one. Kayleigh realized it was the woman she had seen through the window—the woman she'd assumed was Mrs. O'Neill's daughter.

"Don't be alarmed, lass. I'm still me," the woman said. Kayleigh closed her eyes and realized the woman's voice matched Mrs. O'Neill's in rhythm and inflection, but the intonation seemed more youthful. "Only a much younger version."

Kayleigh opened her eyes and took a few shaky breaths. She willed the fear coursing through her to subside, but she still pressed her back against the wall and prepared herself to run.

"Actually," the woman said. "I should say that this is the real me, and the person you knew was an older version of myself. Or how I imagined I might be forty years from now." She adjusted her clothing and flipped her fingers through her hair, twirling a few honey-colored pieces around her finger to curl them away from her eyes. She kicked off her shoes and sat on a chaise, her feet tucked underneath her. "Please do sit before you faint, dearie."

"Who are you?" A dab of apprehension poked at the back of Kayleigh's head, although she perceived she was in no real danger. The woman seemed calm and welcoming.

"It's still me. Anne O'Neill. Your mother's cousin. Although I prefer that you call me Anne when I'm not in morphed form. Mrs. O'Neill makes me feel old."

"How did you do that?" Kayleigh asked. She crossed the foyer and entered the sitting room, but she cut a wide path around the sofa. Fear prevented her from getting too close.

"The same way you do," she said. "I morphed."

"Oh, no, I don't morph." Kayleigh shook her head, tossing her hair across her face.

"You do. The last time we spoke I saw the shimmer on your skin," Anne said.

"Not on purpose, anyway. I gave myself double Ds by accident. Popped right out of my Halloween costume, just because I wished I had more curves."

Anne laughed, and her fair skin flushed with vibrant pink hues. A pang of longing sliced through Kayleigh's chest. Her mother used to laugh as freely, and this woman, her mother's cousin, reminded Kayleigh of what she missed.

"Please, sit with me," Anne said. "You must have many questions."

There were two mahogany leather chairs by the window, deep and comfortable. Kayleigh perched on the edge, not yet sure she wanted to relax her guard.

"When...how...a morph?" Kayleigh stammered. A chill settled over her as the perspiration evaporated off her skin, making her shoulders shake.

"I went through the metamorphosis when I turned thirteen," Anne said. "Imagine your body changing for puberty—acne, hair, breasts—and at the same time you can change your entire appearance. There is no time to get used to one change without the other. We lived in a small village, but neighbors did notice when my hair grew several inches in one day, and I filled out my bra overnight."

Kayleigh laughed and the memory of Halloween night once again popped into her head. Her cheeks warmed, and she nodded.

Anne chuckled and shook her head, the amber curls bouncing around her face. "My mother grabbed my ear and shook me until I morphed back to myself. It's so hard to discover who you really are when you can be anyone. I quickly learned the power was not to be abused. Your mom, on the other hand, was much more mischievous."

"My mother was a morph?" Kayleigh's eyes widened and surprise rippled through her.

"Your mother was quite the morph. She mastered her powers quickly and often went into the village as other people. To her it was the ultimate performance with the best costume. I remember her mother, my Aunt Maud, would say, 'Not in public, Órla!'"

Kayleigh frowned. It was hard to imagine her mother morphing in order to trick people, although she had kept her abilities a secret from her only daughter. Leaving cryptic notes for Kayleigh to find after she went missing didn't seem fair.

"Don't worry. She never did anything mean," Anne said. "She didn't use her morphing abilities to deceive people for anything more than her own fun. Simply to see how they would react to her different personas."

Kayleigh let out a whoosh of relief, and her body sank into the leather chair.

"She seemed to be trying to identify who she really was by trying on everybody else first." Anne sighed and bit her bottom lip. "I was more cautious, I guess. I saw the dark applications of our powers."

"Was my mom taken because of being a morph?" Kayleigh asked.

"I'm afraid so," Anne said. "She believed that morphs should embrace their powers, like any musical ability or athleticism."

"You mean publicly?" Kayleigh asked. She couldn't imagine everyone in school knowing she had the power to look like anybody she wanted.

"Possibly. Your mother became more vocal in morph circles about us being less secretive. I don't think she was ready to go public yet, but she thought that one day morphs could live openly—"

"And someone must not have liked what she was saying." Kayleigh connected the dots, and it seemed like the room suddenly dropped several degrees.

Anne nodded. "I think she saw the best in people and believed that morphing would be an asset to society. Imagine a morph that was particularly skilled at morphing into aquatic mammals like dolphins or whales. They could do marine research or help with search and rescue teams when ships go missing."

"But people don't see the best in each other." Kayleigh thought of cruel people like Emma, who made fun of others for sport.

"No," Anne said. "People often fear what they don't understand or what intimidates them."

"How many morphs are there?" Kayleigh suddenly remembered the genealogy in her mother's chest, which depicted at least part of the family tree back to the Children of Lir.

"Possibly hundreds in different branches of the family tree. It's complicated. Not every generation has a morph, and sometimes there won't be a morph for a hundred years, and then several will be born together. But it seems that both males and females have a chance to inherit the ability to morph — it's a recessive gene."

"You started morphing at thirteen. Why didn't I start morphing until fifteen?" Kayleigh asked.

"I'm not sure, probably because of the influence of your father's genes. The powers kick in around puberty give or take a couple of years."

Kayleigh shifted in her chair and brushed the hair out of her eyes. The mention of puberty and developing powers made her wrinkle her nose.

"I'd rather not have come into my powers." Kayleigh sighed, and the backs of her eyes burned.

"It can be a wonderful gift, Kayleigh," Anne said.

"A gift that malfunctions and scares me." She rubbed her eyes and ran her fingers along the lines of her forehead to smooth out the furrow. This conversation was draining her energy like too many apps on a cell phone drained the battery.

"I can teach you to control it," Anne said.

Kayleigh considered this. Avoidance battled in her head with logic and common sense. Maybe she could learn to control it, or maybe she'd turn into something she couldn't control. Fear won.

Kayleigh stood and edged towards the front door, the urge to flee building in her like a tsunami about to crash into shore. "No way. I'm not ready, and I'll probably screw everything up. I'll make everything worse."

"You can learn." Anne rose and put her hands out in front of her as if encouraging Kayleigh to wait.

"Someone kidnapped my mother for being a morph. I miss her. I want her back." Kayleigh's voice rose in both volume and pitch, fear overwhelming her. "How do I know they're not coming after me just because we're having this conversation?" Her breathing became labored and fresh sweat broke out on her brow. Kayleigh glanced out the window, already paranoid someone might have followed her.

"Kayleigh, you don't have to be afraid."

"You're wrong." Kayleigh opened the front door, stepped outside, and glanced back at the woman who had un-aged forty years in seconds. "If my mother had been afraid, maybe she'd still be here."

Later that week, Kayleigh pulled her English book out of her locker and shut the door. It closed with a *clang* as the lock snapped into place. She glanced down the hallway filled with students—slamming lockers, laughing, stomping on the floor—but none of these sounds registered in her head. There was a roaring ocean of questions and confusion crashing around her skull, drowning out thoughts about school.

She was ostensibly going through the motions of being a student — getting books, following along in class, doing homework — but everything ran on autopilot. Her mind wasn't absorbing any new information, only replaying the meeting with the real Anne O'Neill.

She remembered the first time the elderly version of Anne, Mrs. O'Neill, had come by their house. She brought a casserole and told a story of how she had recently moved in and heard about their misfortune. Lies.

The few seconds it took for Mrs. O'Neill to morph back into her true form played in slow motion in Kayleigh's mind. White hair exchanged for strawberry blonde, age spots switched for freckles, wrinkles swapped for smooth skin. Kayleigh's temples began to throb as she thought again about those several seconds that had solidly confirmed to her that morphs existed.

She had lain in bed at night and imagined her mother learning to morph, pretending to be someone else, running around the hills of Ireland. Sunshine and laughter permeated those memories. When she did sleep, those dreams turned to nightmares as she pictured an older version of her mother talking loudly, boldly enough to get herself snatched by angry, evil morphs with shifting faces.

The nightmare of running in the classrooms at school returned, only this time men chased her. She could hear her mother's voice, calling for help, somewhere inside the school, but Kayleigh ran and ran, never finding her mother and never escaping the men determined to hunt her down.

Resentment simmered deep in Kayleigh. She was angry her mother hadn't kept her mouth shut about morphs living publically and hadn't been able to stay to care for her daughter. Instead she'd gotten herself kidnapped. Taken away. She should have been there to help her only daughter through The Change.

Grief from her mother's disappearance could have delayed Kayleigh's change. The shock of coming home to a trashed house surely put stress on her mind and body. Hyperarousal or PTSD or whatever Mrs. Rouhani and Mr. Stanley were saying. Or maybe with her father's Latino blood, she didn't really become a woman until she turned fifteen. *La Quinceñera.* Yet even after completing puberty, she still didn't feel like anything more than a scared little girl.

Fear grew within her whenever Kayleigh thought about the people who took her mother. Were they really even morphs trying to keep her quiet, or were they humans who meant all morphs harm? People who would trash a house and beat up a defenseless man clearly were not above using violence to get what they wanted. To what lengths would they go to keep her mother quiet, including endangering her daughter?

Back in the present, Kayleigh walked through the hallway in a fog. Students jostled her in their rush to get to class, but she continued to plod down the corridor, caught up in the battle that waged inside her own head.

Chirp chirp. Nonys signaled their arrival to over half the cell phones in the hallway. Kayleigh snapped to attention, and the haze lifted. *Not again.*

She pulled out her phone and opened the Nony app. Around her, students began to snicker.

Anonymous: Seen any good pictures lately, Kayleigh?

Another copy of the photo Emma had posted on her Me3 page accompanied the Nony, only someone had photoshopped a skeleton into her image, making her seem like the living dead.

A few students did gasp, although the majority assumed it was still a joke. Students nudged each other and took out their phones. Kayleigh's head became dizzy, and the room moved in circles.

Get it together. Do not faint.

Kayleigh pushed past several students and grabbed the doorknob to English class.

The door swung open, and Kayleigh dropped the knob and took a step back to avoid being hit in the face.

"Careful with the—" Kayleigh stopped dead when she came face to face with Emma.

"Door?" Emma asked. Her lip curled up into a sneer. Kayleigh took another step back. Students spilled into the hallway. "Why don't you watch where you're going, or aren't you done skipping class, yet?"

"What?" Kayleigh asked. She looked around at her classmates who had exited English class. Students stopped to take in the show, and the corridor filled with onlookers.

"We know the excuse to go to the nurse is bogus," Emma said. "You just like to visit that Mexican woman." Emma placed both hands on her hips and leaned forward, using her height to tower over Kayleigh.

"Mrs. Rouhani is from Iran, actually," Kayleigh said. She tried to take another step back and bumped into a throng of students. She shifted the backpack over her shoulder and tried to wedge a hole between bodies to escape.

"Iran, Mexico, whatever," Emma said.

Kayleigh found herself surrounded by students with Emma mere inches away from her face. Trapped. Her cheeks burned and a cold shiver of fear traveled down her back. She glanced around and saw Bridget standing on the other side of the circle. Bridget had her arms out, gesturing, motioning for Kayleigh to do something to defend herself.

Kayleigh wanted to run, but she knew she had to stand up for herself at some point. Emma continued to taunt her with a singsong voice, poking her, daring her. The other students had started to chant, "Fight fight."

If only I were as tall as Bridget, she couldn't intimidate me anymore. The strange sensation vibrated through Kayleigh's feet as anger coursed through her muscles. Her feet pushed on the edges of her shoes, and tremors of warmth moved up her calves. Kayleigh recognized her legs changing and lengthening.

Wait, no, not this way. Kayleigh wanted to stand up to Emma — but not quite so literally. She couldn't risk morphing in front of others. *Use words.*

Kayleigh opened her mouth to speak, and Emma held up a hand to quiet the crowd.

"Did you want to say something?" Emma's voice dripped with contempt.

Kayleigh's breath escaped from her mouth with a soft whoosh. The only word that came to mind was morph. An awkward silence fell over the crowd.

Chirp chirp. The Nony notification began chirping on phones, and as more students fished their phones out of pockets and purses, the chittering crescendoed, its piercing ring sending waves of dread throughout her body.

Kayleigh's hands trembled as she peered at the phone. Emma pulled her phone out of the pocket of her jeans, one eyebrow raised in curiosity.

Anonymous: How about you faint again, only this time you die?

The Nony hit her like two punches in the stomach. Kayleigh read the emotions of the crowd — surprise, pity, glee.

"Hah, someone else that loathes you as much as I do," Emma said.

The crowd became silent. Kayleigh looked around the circle, staring at the faces of her classmates. Many had their phones in their hands, glancing back and forth between Kayleigh and Emma.

"Excuse me," Kayleigh said. She pushed past Emma and plowed through the students down the hall, chased by peals of Emma's laughter.

"Kayleigh, wait," Bridget called after her.

Kayleigh turned the corner at the end of the hall and burst into the girls' room. She ran the faucet and splashed cold water on her face. Tears mixed with water and ran down her cheeks, dropping into the basin.

Bridget slammed open the lavatory door. It swung closed behind her with a crash. "Kayleigh, what happened?" She checked all the stalls, probably to make sure they were alone. "Why didn't you fight back?"

"I tried, but I started to morph. I wished I was taller, and then I could actually feel my legs getting longer."

"I get that morphing in front of a hallway full of students is not the best idea." Bridget's face was hard, her words harsh. "But why not just shout at Emma, push her out of your face or something resembling standing up for yourself?"

A chill washed over Kayleigh as she listened to Bridget rant about her not being more assertive. The barrage of her words continued, each syllable poking Kayleigh's skin like bee stings. She felt small and helpless against her friend's anger, which was sharper and more damaging than Emma's taunts.

Kayleigh sagged back against the wall and sank to the floor. She covered her ears and tried to curl into a ball. A shiver raced over her skin, and she shuddered as she began to morph. Her skin shimmered and shrank in on itself. As her body became smaller, her sweater hung off her shoulders. Her shoes were several sizes too big. She recoiled from Bridget's words both physically and emotionally.

"Kayleigh, stop shrinking!" Bridget grabbed her friend's hands and pulled her away from the wall, hauling her to her feet and giving her a hard shake. Kayleigh caught her reflection in the mirror and saw that fully standing, she only reached Bridget's waist. *No, this can't be happening.*

Another surge of energy seized her, and she burst through her skin and morphed back to her full size. Her whole body gushed and sparkled as she fought to find her form. *Be Kayleigh, be me.* Her feet became solid again underneath her, and her frame stopped its undulation. When her limbs felt firm, she lunged at Bridget, pushed her to the floor, and charged towards the exit.

Kayleigh slammed into the door and pushed it outward until it crashed into the wall on the other side. The blood roared in her ears, and her breathing came in shallow bursts. All she could think about was how to escape. *Too many doors, no windows.*

Kayleigh bolted down the main hallway towards the front of the school. Only a few stragglers remained, most students already in class. Her boots pounded on the floor, and with each contact against the hard tile, thuds echoed against the metal lockers.

She reached the entrance and pressed the bars on the main doors. Her head pounded, and her lungs begged for air, as if she had swum underwater the entire length of a pool. She tore through the doors and into the cold. The frosty air smacked her in the face and stung her eyes. She took ragged breaths and fought back the blackness that threatened to engulf her in its oblivion.

She sprinted down the walkway, her feet skating on patches of ice. Snow swirled around her head and dampened her sweater. Without thinking about the fact she had no hat or coat, she took off towards home.

A heavy blanket of gray covered the sky and darkened the afternoon. Layers of snow and ice covered each branch and pine needle on the trees, making an eerie backdrop to the drab buildings that lined the street. Spring was late this year.

Kayleigh kept running, kicking aside mounds of slush and ducking under low hanging branches weighted with precipitation. The freezing air burned her nose, and the inside of her ears began to throb. Tears streamed down her face.

Panic pushed her on at full speed, and within fifteen minutes, she had raced from the school to her street. Kayleigh's muscles strained to slow before reaching her gate, and her right foot slipped on a patch of ice hiding underneath the snow. She slid into the ground, like a baseball player stealing second, and landed hard on her hip.

She yelped at the pain that coursed through her leg and collapsed into the snow at the side of the gate. A dull ache lodged itself in her ribcage, and sobs racked her shoulders. Kayleigh's vision blurred as snow and tears covered her face.

Kayleigh heard a primitive howl and realized she was wailing. Deep cries of sorrow flowed from her throat and ripped past her lips. The events of the past several weeks overwhelmed her — discovering she was a morph, meeting the real Anne O'Neill, being taunted by Emma — it was all too much for her to manage. Fighting with Bridget was the nail in her coffin, and she wept under the weight of so many changes.

From behind her came the voice of her elderly neighbor. "Kayleigh, my dear, what happened?" A gloved hand covered Kayleigh's icy one. Strong arms encircled her torso and pulled her into a sitting position. A swatch of olive tweed swung over her shoulder, and warmth covered her back. She gulped in air. The moisture from her breath condensed with every exhalation and floated into the wintry mix.

Kayleigh blinked, and Mrs. O'Neill's face came into focus. The old woman knelt on the ground next to Kayleigh, and she pulled her under her cloak. The heat of her body warmed Kayleigh's icy skin.

"Come, child. We need to get you indoors before you freeze," Mrs. O'Neill said. She helped Kayleigh up and guided her back through the gate and along the path that led to her house.

Safely inside, Mrs. O'Neill shook her head and morphed back into her true form. She shrugged off her shawl and wrapped it around Kayleigh. Anne led Kayleigh through the kitchen to the family room, where a fire filled the area with light and warmth.

Kayleigh sank into an oversized sofa and pulled another blanket around her. Tears continued to flow down her cheeks, and her shoulders silently heaved. Anne poured a cup of tea and pushed it into Kayleigh's frozen fingers.

"Drink up. Warm yourself," Anne said. She rubbed the tops of Kayleigh's arms and brushed the wet hair from Kayleigh's face. Gradually the sobs subsided, and Kayleigh took a sip of lavender tea. *Mom.* She missed her mother so much the pain swelled in her chest, and she leaned on Anne, her mother's cousin. *My cousin.*

"What can I do to help you?" Anne asked, dropping a kiss onto Kayleigh's forehead.

Kayleigh thought about how afraid she had been for so long—scared to confront Emma, terrified of morphing—and how there were real consequences to inaction. Emma had stomped all over her in public, and Kayleigh had done nothing but run away.

Her passivity had taken a toll. She had let a boy, one who was actually interested in her, slip away. And not fighting back moments ago had cost her a best friend. Bridget had screamed at her to stand up for herself, but Kayleigh had morphed into a simpering child. She knew she had to do something to get hold of her power and her life.

She looked up at the woman who knew how to morph and from whom Kayleigh might learn. The trembling subsided and the urge to flee dissipated. A rush of blood through her limbs gave her strength, and she took a deliberate breath.

"Teach me to morph," Kayleigh said. "I'm ready."

CHAPTER NINE

SECRETS

"You're ready to learn how to control your powers?" Anne asked. She smiled down at Kayleigh and stroked her hair, still wet from her fall in the snow.

"I can't keep running anymore," Kayleigh said. "I'm tired of crying non-stop."

"I imagine it's not fun to be so afraid."

"I want to jump out of my skin half the time, and the other half I feel like a zombie—only functioning on a basic level that isn't pretty." Kayleigh smiled wryly and ran a hand through her hair, her fingers catching on knots and tangles.

She sat in silence for several minutes, drinking the tea that Anne had given her. In an effort to prolong the silence, she studied the family room and stared into the huge stone fireplace. A roaring blaze in the hearth cast flickering light across the walls.

Anne finally broke the silence. "It sounds like you have more going on than mere morphing."

"The school psychologist and the nurse both think I have PTSD from two years ago—finding the house trashed, Dad hurt, Mom missing—and that makes me hypervigilant or hyperaroused. Or both." Kayleigh sighed and tried to remember what they had said, but her memory seemed foggy. "Hyper-something. I thought PTSD was for soldiers returning from war, but apparently it can happen to anyone who has experienced trauma."

"It must have been awful to return home and see what they did to your father. You must have been so scared. I bet I would have felt unsafe in my own house."

"It was horrible, but I don't think it hit me at first. When Emma started picking on me again, all the feelings came flooding back: fear, unease, anxiety."

"Emma's a girl at school?"

"A mean girl. The worst. I don't understand what her deal is. She torments me and laughs, seeming to get pleasure out of making me feel bad."

Anne smiled. "Would you like to know a secret?"

Kayleigh hesitated, curious as to where she was taking this but nodded.

"Bullies are actually insecure," Anne said. "They can't be content with who they are, so they put down others to make themselves feel better."

Oh, well she knew that. Kayleigh frowned. "That's what all the adults say, usually when they want you to ignore the ignorant bullies and go on your way." She let out a long breath and chuckled. "That would require victims like me to be secure enough in themselves to just smile and keep walking."

"You don't feel good about yourself?" Anne asked.

"Does anybody?" Kayleigh asked. "I've got zits, frizzy hair, one boob that's growing faster than the other, a weird freckle—"

"And then add in morphing powers," Anne laughed and smoothed a lock of russet hair behind Kayleigh's ear. "It's a perfect storm for a panic attack like the one you had." After fixing Kayleigh's hair, she reached up and tucked one of her amber curls behind her own ear. She smiled, and the resemblance to her mother struck Kayleigh at her core.

Kayleigh wiped the remaining moisture from her cheeks. She savored her tea's healing warmth, breathing in its floral aroma.

"So teach me to fight back," Kayleigh said.

"Morphing isn't exactly a weapon."

"I know. It's not like I'll disguise myself as a tree and sneak up on Emma on the sidewalk—wait, a tree!"

A memory flashed in her mind—a large fern glimmering in the sunlight as she walked through her wrecked home. A fern that hadn't been there before, and which she couldn't recall in the aftermath.

Kayleigh grabbed Anne's hands and gazed directly into her eyes. Excitement crested within her as she put together another piece of the puzzle. "Can someone disguise themselves as a tree?"

"It's possible, but it's tricky," Anne said. "Usually morphing into such a detailed organism as a plant leaves a telltale sheen around the morph."

Kayleigh's heart hammered in her chest. "That's what I saw—the shimmer of a morph. I ran right into a solid object as I ran through the house looking for my father. After it knocked me down, I saw a strange plant in the corner. It was a fern, but the colors were off. It was blurry, and the edges shined a bit."

Anne sat up straight, and her eyes widened. "You ran into a morph?"

"I think so. Later the plant was gone, but a cleaning service had come in and straightened the entire house, so I didn't think about it until now."

"I'm so glad you're okay." Anne gave Kayleigh another hug and rested her chin on the top of her head. "I didn't realize you were so close to the kidnappers."

"Why didn't they take me, too?" Kayleigh asked.

"You hadn't come into your powers yet," Anne said. "And you weren't talking about morphs revealing themselves to humans. So you were only a normal little girl then and no threat to them."

"Normal," Kayleigh said. She dropped into the hug and let Anne's strong arms support her weight. "What's that?"

Anne pulled back and put a hand on each side of Kayleigh's face. "I should have said typical — that you were a typical girl at that time. And now you are an extraordinary young woman. Atypical in a good way." She smiled and studied Kayleigh's face. "So much like your mother. I miss her very much."

"Me too."

Anne patted her knee and stood. "You must be hungry. I'll fix us some lunch, and we should probably let the school know you're okay."

A rush of guilt knocked Kayleigh over. She remembered fighting with Bridget and then racing out of the school, leaving her coat and backpack behind. Her English teacher must have wondered what happened to her. "I wonder if the school called my dad."

"With a few phone calls, we'll get it all straightened out...for now." She winked at Kayleigh and walked into the kitchen. The family room and kitchen were separated by a breakfast bar and counters, but otherwise open. One ceiling flowed over both rooms, and two rows of exposed beams in a dark wood formed a triangle at the top, creating a rustic look. The cozy vibe made Kayleigh relax. *I'm safe.*

For the next twenty minutes, Anne chatted with the school and Kayleigh's father. From the one-sided conversation, it seemed they had been concerned about her. Anne reassured them that she was fine and safe as she multitasked, arranging sandwiches and cookies on a tray.

Anne came back to the sofa, balancing the platter of food and a pitcher of iced tea. "Okay, dearie, let's get you fed, and then we'll make a plan."

Kayleigh picked up a finger sandwich, while Anne added another log to the fire. A row of large windows spanned one side of the room, looking onto the garden. Although a blanket of wet snow dripped off the trees and dampened the plants, various shapes and sizes of foliage decorated the back yard. A small wrought iron table and chairs, now covered in a dusting of ice, sat in the middle, surrounded by a ring of small bushes. A tall wooden fence, covered with English ivy, surrounded the whole yard. It was Anne's secret garden.

"Too bad we can't have tea outside right now," Kayleigh said. "Your garden looks peaceful."

"It'll warm up in a couple of weeks," Anne said. "You know what they say about March. In like a lion—"

"Out like a lamb." Kayleigh finished the sentence for her. "I've certainly felt the roar so far."

Anne chuckled. "When the weather warms, we'll go out to the garden to train."

"Train?"

"There are several principles of morphing that you must master."

"What kinds of principles?"

"They teach you how to manage your mind, your emotions, and your physical body, including your actions. All three are interconnected, and in order to morph successfully, you must have an understanding of them all."

"That sounds complicated." Kayleigh finished a sandwich and washed it down with iced tea. This was sounding more and more like school.

"It gets easier with time, like any skill."

"Who taught you?"

A melancholy look stole over Anne's face, and her eyes dropped to her left hand. A silver band circled her ring finger with the Celtic never-ending knot. Upon first glance it seemed like several intertwining loops, but in reality it was one thread wound around and around.

"My husband did," Anne said.

"You were married?"

"I was once. He was also a morph, and he helped me perfect my powers before he died," Anne twisted the ring on her finger, and her eyes misted with tears.

Kayleigh wanted to ask how he died, but that seemed like too personal a question. She wondered how they had met, and more generally, how one morph recognized another. New questions about how to control morphing powers flooded her mind.

"So what's the first lesson?" Kayleigh asked.

"Let's take it one step at a time. Rest and get a good night's sleep before we start training," Anne said. "Your dad's waiting at home for you."

Dad. Another rush of guilt swept through Kayleigh. She'd been avoiding any significant conversation with him since he'd seen her mother's necklace around her neck. They had to talk at some point; she couldn't keep saying she was tired and then retreat to her room, and he couldn't continue to say he had papers to grade in his study.

She bade Anne goodbye and borrowed a coat to cross the short distance between their two houses. The wind picked up and tossed the branches on the trees. Heavy clumps of snow dropped to the sidewalk, and icicles dislodged from the roofs, raining down like knives.

Kayleigh walked around the front of her house, wondering if her father was in his study or the kitchen. She had a 50-50 chance of entering on the opposite side of the house from him, which meant more time to hide. The front door of their two-story colonial sat closer to his study, whereas the mudroom door on the side adjoined the kitchen and family room.

Since it was still early afternoon, she chose the mudroom door on the other side of the house. She entered, and a blast of warm air scented with chicken soup tickled her nose. She hesitated by the benches when she caught sight of her hat and coat. Someone had brought them home after school.

A low murmur of voices emanated from behind the door that led to the kitchen. Kayleigh froze, and remorse warmed her cheeks. The someone who brought her things was still here. She briefly considered taking the door into the family room and running upstairs, but that was definitely a door she tried to avoid ever since she'd pushed it open two years ago and left behind the last traces of a normal life.

She pressed her ear against the smooth wood of the door leading to the kitchen. The familiar rumble of her father's voice conversed with a female voice, one that spoke slowly and with equal stress on each syllable—Mrs. Rouhani.

Kayleigh pushed open the door and paused when she saw her father and the nurse sitting at the kitchen table. The contents of the crockpot simmered underneath the glass top, emitting the aroma of chicken, noodles, and vegetables. Steam rose from the teapot on the stove, and a tin container of Persian chai tea sat on the counter.

"Kayleigh, *Joon*," Mrs. Rouhani said. "I'm so glad you made it home okay."

"Yeah," Kayleigh said. The corners of her lips pinched together, and she didn't move from the door, suspicious to see the nurse in her kitchen. She relied on Ms. Rouhani at school but wasn't sure how she felt about having her in their home.

"Come in," her father said. "Soraya was nice enough to bring your things home from school and fill me in on what happened."

"Do school nurses make house calls?" Wariness leaked into her voice.

"Katherine Leigh, don't be rude," her father said.

"Cedro, it's okay." Mrs. Rouhani smiled at him and placed a hand over his arm. She quickly withdrew and stood, flipping her thick braid over her shoulder. "Why don't I pour you some tea? It's a chai infused with rose petals that I brought from Iran for your father."

"No, thank you, I had lavender tea at Mrs. O'Neill's house." Kayleigh continued to stand rooted to the floor at the edge of the kitchen. Alarm bells clanged in her head, alerting her to the intimate atmosphere between her father and a woman who wasn't her mother. "What's going on here?"

Mrs. Rouhani sat back down and paused before speaking. "Several students came to my office at school to tell me what happened in the hallway with Emma. They showed me the pictures that were posted on her Me3 page and the one on the Nony site."

"I remember the bullying. I'm not confused about that. I mean what's happening *here*," Kayleigh said, emphasizing the last word and gesturing between the two adults.

Her father cleared his throat. "Soraya and I have been...friends for a while. She brought me your things and told me what happened."

"Friends?" Kayleigh's eyes narrowed as she studied the two adults. Mrs. Rouhani blushed and averted her eyes under Kayleigh's scrutiny.

"I should go," Mrs. Rouhani said. She rose and grabbed her coat from where it lay next to her on the bench. "You need time to talk with your daughter." Emilio rubbed against her legs, purring.

"I'll walk you to the door," her father said. He placed a hand on the small of Mrs. Rouhani's back and guided her through the family room to the front door. Kayleigh slunk around the kitchen isle and watched them until they disappeared into the front foyer. The front door opened with a pop, and all the doors between the kitchen and family room shifted from the change in air pressure that rippled throughout the house.

Emilio wandered back and plopped on the floor with a yawn. He studied her with a typical apathetic feline gaze.

"Traitor," she told him.

Kayleigh meandered to the kettle and pulled open the top to look at the chai tea. Unlike her mother's light lavender tea, which had a golden color and bright smell, Mrs. Rouhani's tea appeared dark and spiced. There were black leaves and textured seeds floating in the water. She leaned her head over and inhaled deeply, but she could only identify the faint scent of roses. An image of gilded doors rimmed in turquoise and topped with pointed arches in a desert marketplace jumped into her mind.

"There was no need to be rude," her father said, entering the kitchen. "She's been very kind to you."

"At *school*. I didn't expect her to be at my house."

"*Our* house, and she is also my friend. I expect you to be polite."

"What kind of friends are you, exactly?" Kayleigh placed the lid back on the kettle and moved to inspect the crock pot bubbling with golden broth. A warm gush of steam scented with poultry flooded her nose and opened her sinuses.

"What do you mean?" her father asked.

"I first saw you in the nurse's office after I fainted," Kayleigh said. She turned down the heat on the soup and replaced the glass top. She glared at her father. "You used Mrs. Rouhani's first name, and when she put her hand on your arm you put your hand over hers. It was way too cozy for friends."

"I respect Soraya. I enjoy her company. She's caring and intelligent." Her father leaned on the other side of the kitchen island—the tea, soup, and a great emotional distance—stood between them. "And yes, we've gone out on several...dates."

"You've what?" Kayleigh rounded the island and took a step towards her father but changed her mind and retreated to the wooden table. The muscles of her shoulders bunched into knots, and her gut twisted and turned on itself. A woozy feeling forced her to sit down. She plopped at the kitchen table, her back to her father. "How could you do that to Mom?"

"Your mother's been gone for two and a half years," her father said. "I loved her with all my heart. I think I'll always love her."

"Then, how could you cheat on her?" Kayleigh shifted the full force of her gaze to his. Fat tears welled in her eyes and hovered on the edge of her lashes, like water forming a meniscus on the rim of a glass too full. One more drop, and the seal would be broken.

"It's not cheating. Your mother's gone, and although I do still love her, I need companionship and love in the present. I can't cling to a dying hope that she'll return one day."

"Mom is alive. I know it." Kayleigh tried to scream in frustration but only managed a strangled yelp. She swiveled on the bench to face him more directly. "I am going to find her. I will."

"You are so much like your mother. She was always stubborn and headstrong."

"And a morph!" Kayleigh blurted. She gasped and clapped her hands to her mouth before she said anything more. Anne had told her that the people took her mother because she was too outspoken, and now Kayleigh might have put her father in danger again by revealing this secret to him.

Her father slowly walked to the table and eased himself down onto a bench opposite Kayleigh. He took in shaky breaths and released them in a controlled, methodical manner. Kayleigh tried to read his face — was that anger?

He took another breath and finally spoke. "I know."

Kayleigh's mouth dropped open with surprise, and her eyes widened. Her breath caught in the back of her throat. A whirlwind of conflicting emotions swirled in her chest — shock, relief, and betrayal.

"You knew?" The sharp pain of knowledge punched Kayleigh in the gut like a heavyweight boxer. Her shoulders sank into her ribs, and her chin dropped to her chest. "And you never told me?"

"Your mother got herself into trouble by being too candid about morphs, and I didn't want anything to happen to you. But I've always known." He dropped his head into his hands, and his voice became soft.

Kayleigh picked up her head, straining her neck muscles. Her back protested. She narrowed her gaze on his face, concentrating on his words.

"She told me when we were dating," he continued. "I was already so in love with her that I didn't care. I think I thought it was a parlor trick, maybe. I didn't understand the implications of my wife being a morph until they…whoever they are…took her. Then, it was too late. She was gone."

"How could you keep that secret from me?" Kayleigh rose from the table and paced the length of the kitchen. She pivoted at the opposite end, wrung her hands, and shook her head. She plodded back, betrayal seeping into her like a stain on her favorite sweater — ugly and permanent.

"You accuse me of keeping a secret?" Her father stood, and his frame tensed up and become rigid. "Katherine Leigh Paz-Purcell. I know you are like your mother in the most serious of ways, and you kept it a secret from me."

At the other end of the kitchen, Kayleigh stopped mid-pivot and stared at her father. A gulp of air caught in her throat, and her whole body tensed. "What do you mean?"

"You are a morph, just like your mother." His hands formed fists at his sides, and his face had lost its warmth and understanding. It was his turn to throw icy accusations.

"How did you know?" Kayleigh couldn't move, her feet filled with cement, plastered to the floor.

"I saw you start to change. In the nurse's office at school," he said. "I'd seen that same shimmer in your mother when she morphed."

"Why didn't you say something?" Kayleigh asked. Her knees suddenly buckled underneath her, and she sank to the tiles. Any remaining energy drained from her body, and the strain of today's events caught up to her. She had run a marathon and collapsed before she had reached the end. She had struggled on her own for all these months, while her father had known what was happening.

How could he let her suffer like that?

He left the table and knelt. He placed a hand on her shoulder and gently squeezed. "I couldn't confirm that you were actually getting powers. You didn't seem to know what was happening and didn't actually morph. I hoped your power was defective and wouldn't actually develop."

"Defective," Kayleigh repeated. She slumped back against the kitchen wall, and the smooth stone tile of the kitchen floor beneath her legs chilled her bottom through her jeans, which still hadn't dried completely from her afternoon sprint through the snow. She looked at her father, and her eyes widened. "Completely defective. At the Halloween dance, I accidentally gave myself big boobs."

"You gave yourself big boo—ah, yes?" Her father's face reddened, and he coughed and cleared his throat. He shifted off his knees and sat next to her against the wall. "How...inconvenient?"

"I can't deny wanting more on top," Kayleigh said, looking down at her small curves. "Wishing them into existence without warning was not what I had in mind, though."

"I'm sorry," he said, and a chuckle escaped his lips. Kayleigh's face flushed, but she couldn't help but giggle herself. He cleared his throat again but Kayleigh still saw a grin play at the corners of his mouth.

"What did you do?" he asked.

"I ran away to the locker room. I've never been so embarrassed. I'd actually broken the laces on my dress." Laughter piled up in her belly and spilled out her mouth in giggles and hiccups. Her father joined in, his low chuckles shaking his shoulders.

"And to make matters worse, I then started to turn into a swan like my costume." Kayleigh let her head fall back against the wall, tears spilling over onto her cheeks. Her side began to ache from laughing so hard.

"I hope it wasn't a swan with big boo—"

"Dad!" Kayleigh gasped and smacked her father on the arm.

"I'm sorry, again. I never heard these kinds of stories from your mother, and I never thought I'd be having this kind of conversation with my daughter." His laughter subsided, and he threw an arm around Kayleigh.

"Being a teenager is so much harder nowadays than it was for me," he said. "Technology alone makes it seem like you're growing up in a spotlight of sorts, everyone weighing in with their comments and criticism."

"And then add in turning into a morph."

"And losing your mother."

"Put it all together, and it's been the adolescence from he—"

"Hey, let's not add in swearing," her father said, once again the proper professor.

Kayleigh sighed and leaned her head against the arm still encircling her shoulders. For all the arguing—and laughing—she and her father seemed to be doing lately, this was the closest she had ever felt to him. Her mother's disappearance had previously lowered the temperature in the house several degrees. Not down to a total cold war, for Kayleigh knew that she and her father got along far better than some teenagers and their parents. Both sides had kept secrets, however, and the situation wasn't improved by the introduction of Mrs. Rouhani into her father's life.

The kitchen looked different from where they sat. The center island towered, covered in granite and imposing, and the wooden table seemed like a dry forest of thick branches. Kayleigh leaned into her father, trying to ward off a chill. Outside the March wind howled and pushed against the house, making the windows creak in their casings. Tufts of snow slid off of the roof and streaked past the glass.

"Come on," her father said. He pushed himself off the floor and stood, offering her a hand. "Let's eat some soup."

"Okay." Kayleigh accepted his hand and let him pull her to her feet. "But no more tea." She smiled and gave him a hug. "Or secrets."

He pulled her close, and his arms tightened around her shoulders. "It's a deal."

CHAPTER TEN

MIND

S pring break finally arrived several weeks later, and Kayleigh could get away from the house without drawing complaints from her father about homework. The first day of vacation, Kayleigh rose at her usual time, although instead of school, she went to visit Anne O'Neill again.

Kayleigh grabbed a light jacket, the weather having warmed into the sixties the first several days of April. She crossed the short distance between the two yards at a jog. She rang the bell and rocked back and forth on her feet, trying to expel some of the nervous energy oozing from her pores. Today was the day she'd begin training to be a morph. Or if she were already technically a morph, today she would hopefully learn how to not be a walking accident.

"Good morning, dearie." The elderly Mrs. O'Neill opened the door and scanned the front yard and street as she motioned for Kayleigh to enter. Mrs. O'Neill closed the heavy oak door with a thud, stepped away from the slim windows that flanked the entrance, and morphed out of her older persona and back into Anne. In an instant, she lost forty years, at least that many pounds, and a radiant smile appeared on her face. Anne gave Kayleigh a hug, squeezing her tightly. The scent of vanilla and jasmine washed over her as comforting as her mother's lavender.

"Sorry I answered the door in disguise," Anne said. "I can't be sure there aren't people watching me…or you."

An icy chill rippled down Kayleigh's spine, and she peered out of the elongated stained glass on one side of the door and wondered who might be staring at the house, perhaps from the other side of the street in disguise or shrouded in shadows.

"I didn't mean to make you nervous, lass. Come in, please." She took Kayleigh's jacket and hung it in the hall closet. "It's been well over two years since they took your mum, and no one new has shown up in your life, right? So I think we're safe."

"Anyone new?" Kayleigh asked. "What do you mean?"

"Well, if you had a suspicious mind. It might have been too coincidental for you that I arrived immediately after your mum disappeared."

"But you were such a nice old lady—I mean, elderly neighbor."

"That's true, but morphs can disguise themselves as anyone. Old or young, male or female, kind or not." Anne walked into the family room, motioning for Kayleigh to follow.

As she obeyed, she tried to remember back to her thirteenth birthday, the day the house was ransacked. She couldn't recall anyone arriving around that time who might have been suspicious. Of course she did run into a plant that shimmered and moved, but she was too scared in that moment to be suspicious. It had never crossed her mind someone had been spying on her. Kayleigh shivered and tried to rub away the goose bumps prickling her arms.

"Would you like some rashers, eggs, and black pudding?" Anne stopped in the kitchen, where a frying pan of thick bacon sizzled. The aroma made Kayleigh's stomach rumble. She realized she'd skipped breakfast in her rush to start training.

"Yes, please. It smells wonderful." Kayleigh sat on one of the barstools lining the far side of the island. For the next few minutes, she watched Anne finish the bacon, prepare several eggs sunny side up, and butter slices of a pale brown bread. She took another pat of butter and dropped it in a pan with some potato wedges and rounds of black sausage. Kayleigh closed her eyes and inhaled the scents of an Irish breakfast. A memory of her mother preparing food floated into her mind.

"I thought you were preparing pudding," a five-year-old Kayleigh said.

"I am." Her mother laughed and flipped over black circles in a frying pan. Her red hair shone as bright as a fire engine in the light streaming through the window.

"It doesn't look like pudding."

"That's because it's black pudding."

"But I eat pudding with a spoon." Kayleigh put her elbows on the table and dropped her chin onto her hands, a pout forming on her lips.

"Black pudding is actually blood sausage."

"Ew, blood?" Kayleigh sat up and shook her head. "I'm not eating that."

"You'll give it a try, and you'll see how yummy it is."

Her mother had been right. Kayleigh had liked black pudding and had learned to try new things. She missed her mother's assurance and how she encouraged her to take risks. She watched Anne as she plated the food, a hearty breakfast to get her through this next big challenge.

After they ate, Anne laid a green patchwork quilt over the carpet and placed two large floor pillows facing each other. She sat on one cross-legged and gestured for Kayleigh to do the same.

Kayleigh took a deep breath. Game time.

Anne placed her hands on her thighs. "There are three main principles of morphing that use the mind, body, and soul. The first lesson of morphing is mindfulness. By being mindful or more aware of your thoughts, emotions, and actions, you'll be able to morph more effectively."

"I only seem to morph when I'm not really paying attention," Kayleigh said. "And then not very well."

"Be patient. Step one is learning mindfulness. It's a way of using your mind purposefully."

"Okay." Kayleigh copied Anne's relaxed posture.

"If you wanted to get into the lotus position, each foot would come up over the knee." Anne demonstrated. "Either way, the idea is that you sit comfortably and breathe deeply. After you master this, you'll be able to be mindful wherever you are and with whatever you're doing."

Anne took several long breaths, inhaling through her nose and exhaling through her mouth. Kayleigh tried to breathe slowly, but a bubble of air caught the back of her throat, and she coughed. She shifted on her bottom and tried to stifle the waves of discomfort that flushed her cheeks.

Anne continued. "The concept of mindfulness originally came from Buddhism, although now it is used not only in spirituality but in psychology as well."

Kayleigh slowed her breathing to match her teacher's. She drew air from deep in her chest and noticed her diaphragm expanding with each breath. Her heart rate slowed, and her muscles relaxed.

"To be mindful means that you accept without judgment any and all feelings you have in the moment," Anne said. "You intentionally focus on all the sensations you may be experiencing in the present."

"What do I do with all the stuff in my head? I have so much going on it becomes overwhelming. I want to try to block it out, not focus on it."

"Don't push those experiences away or cling to them. Merely observe them with the calm detachment of a person watching a movie. Whatever thought might come into your mind or whatever emotion you feel is all part of your present moment and should be accepted."

Kayleigh thought of her present moment. Instead of calm detachment, a barrage of questions swirled around in her head and screamed as loud as bleating goats. *When am I going to learn to morph? Where is my mother? What is Emma planning next? Am I in danger? Can I morph away my acne?*

As these thoughts entered her mind, pangs of anxiety and fear tightened her chest and dampened her palms. Fear and anxiety grew within her like a mushroom cloud of panic. She squeezed her eyes shut and willed them to go away.

"I can see you fighting the 'overwhelm,'" Anne said. "It looks like you tensed up to push away everything you are feeling. The trick is to let whatever thoughts or emotions you experience come into your body, like an ocean wave and then recede exactly like the ocean. Gradually, you will be able to accept those thoughts and feelings rather than fight them. Questions don't need to be answered at this time, simply noted as part of the ocean wave."

Kayleigh focused on Anne's eyes and her soothing presence. She tried to imagine those emotions—fear, anxiety, confusion—as waves, crashing into shore but then washing away. Kayleigh liked the ocean and the rhythmic sloshing of water against the sand.

"Emotions are your body's response to thoughts you have," Anne said. "Accept those feelings for the information they give you, but don't feel like you have to act on that information. You could say to yourself, 'Oh, look, Fear. Fear would like me to run and hide. Well, Fear, I will consider it, but I'm not going to do anything yet, thank you.'"

Kayleigh laughed at Anne's personification of fear. To Kayleigh, fear was a huge black specter in decaying robes that was ready to drag her away if she didn't run and hide. It wasn't something with which she could have a casual conversation.

"Fear always makes me anxious," Kayleigh said. "And then anxiety leads to panic, and panic leads to unfortunate morphing or running and hiding."

"Yes, morphing at an inopportune moment is not the best way to deal with these feelings." Anne smiled and leaned over to light a candle that sat on the fireplace hearth. "Don't be afraid of your fear. Try again."

Kayleigh took a shaky breath and watched the flame gather strength and throw shadows on the wall. A thin stream of smoke snaked upwards toward the beams in the ceiling. A thought immediately popped into her mind. *Who are you, Kayleigh?* Her chest began to tighten, and she looked down at her hands, which trembled slightly on her legs, sending small vibrations along her jeans.

Kayleigh recognized she was reacting to the thought, which made her worried and want to flee. She took a deep breath instead and accepted the emotions as natural. She acknowledged to herself that it was not an unreasonable question. *I don't have the answer just yet, but it's all good.* She imagined the idea floating around in her head like a white fluffy cloud until it gradually faded away. Relief swelled in her chest and rolled over her limbs.

"Good," Anne said. "I can see your shoulders relaxing and the tension draining out of you." She smiled and nodded her head in encouragement. "Once you can let the thoughts and feelings simply happen, you are free to let them *be*, rather than have to *do* anything with them."

"So you want me to be aware of my emotions, but instead of pushing them away or acting on them, I should just observe them?"

"That's right."

"And when do I get to morphing?"

"First things first. Once you're mindful of what's going on inside your body, you can also tune into other things you may have missed."

"Like what?"

"Close your eyes for a moment, and let's tune into our other senses. Touch. Taste. Sound. Smell."

Kayleigh sighed and closed her eyes, concentrating on slowing her breathing. Thoughts scrambled for recognition in her brain, but she let them yell and then grow silent. She stroked her fingers over the worn material of her jeans, the thicker seam running down the outside of her thigh.

Her breath whistled softly as it passed through her nose and the warmth of her exhale tickled the edges of her lips. The pleasing taste of bacon lingered on her tongue. She noticed a faint aroma of sandalwood, which must have come from the candle.

A low hum rumbled in the background, probably from the furnace. The motor of the refrigerator buzzed, and the icemaker released another batch of cubes with a clatter.

The loud caw of a crow from the garden grabbed her attention. Outside, the soft *cheep* of sparrows mixed with the varied calls of a blue jay. Water dripped onto the patio like a leaky faucet, and squirrels chittered. *Spring.*

Kayleigh opened her eyes wide and stared at her mentor. "I've never really noticed so much is happening around me. I knew those sounds existed, for example, but I didn't really pay attention."

"Most of the time our brains filter out much of what we actually receive," Anne said. "Usually because we deem other information more important. Once we lose touch of our surroundings, we blindly react to our thoughts and emotions. We *become* the emotions, and we lose ourselves."

"I don't want to be lost anymore." Kayleigh rocked forward on her knees and threw her arms around Anne's shoulders.

Beep Beep.

Anne pulled back from Kayleigh and looked around the room. "What was that?"

Kayleigh's face flushed, and her shoulders rose to touch her ears. "Sorry, that's a text." She glanced at her bag, and her hands began to tremble.

"Hey." Anne grabbed Kayleigh's fingers. "Mindfulness. Be aware of the thoughts and emotions, but don't let them take you over."

Kayleigh took a deep breath and acknowledged that her pulse raced, and beads of sweat broke out on her forehead. Thoughts scuffled for space in her head, and emotions churned in her gut. *Who is texting me? Is it nasty? Don't answer! Fear. Confusion. Panic.*

She slowly rose and walked to her phone, each footstep bringing her closer to potential ridicule. *Don't assume anything, since that would be thinking into the future. Stay in the present moment. You are safe and loved and just going to look at a piece of technology.*

She slid the phone out of the side pocket of her purse and entered the unlock code. She tried not to hold her breath as the phone brought up the text message.

Nate: happy spring break

Kayleigh let out a whoosh of air and turned to smile at Anne.

"It's my boy…male friend. I mean, a friend who is a male. A boy. Nate." Cotton coated Kayleigh's tongue, and she tripped over the words. She wondered if this conversation would have been more or less awkward with her mother.

"A boy you like, obviously." Anne smiled and rose. "I'll give you a minute alone."

"No, don't." Kayleigh jumped up. She grabbed Anne's hand as if it were a lifesaver that could keep her from drowning. "It's just...I'm not sure what to do." She wiped her palms on her jeans and rubbed the end of her shirt across the damp screen.

"Answer him?" Anne asked. She raised one eyebrow and cocked her head.

"I could," Kayleigh said, following her into the kitchen. "But I accidentally blew him off, and I think he may now be dating Hannah."

"He's not." Anne took some iced tea out of the refrigerator and poured two tall glasses.

"How do you know?"

"He wouldn't be texting you if he were dating another girl."

"Theoretically," Kayleigh said. "Not all guys are Boy Scouts." She chuckled and tried to sound casual, but her heart beat like a metronome set on *Allegro*.

"So text him back," Anne said.

Kayleigh looked at the phone and again at Anne, who took a sip of her iced tea and shrugged.

"Sure, why not?" Kayleigh moved her thumbs over the screen.

Kayleigh: thanks, u 2

Nate: whatcha doin?

Kayleigh's head snapped up, and she glanced towards the pillows on the floor and the candle. Not sure how specific to be, she hesitated, not wanting to completely lie either.

Kayleigh: meditating... you?

The few minutes it took for Nate to text back seemed like an eternity. Anne smiled, sipped her tea, and prepared lunch.

Nate: cool, I'm watching tv. w2m l8r?

A flock of butterflies migrated south in her stomach, and Kayleigh plopped on one of the bar stools before her knees gave way. She stared at the phone blankly and froze.

"Well, what did he say?" Anne asked.

"He's asking if I want to meet up later."

"So what's the problem?"

"Nothing, really. Other than I get so nervous every time I'm around him that I want to run or turn myself into something that can float or fly away."

"So try mindfulness," Anne said. "This is a perfect way to practice the first principle of morphing. It's okay to feel freaked out and scared on the inside. Your mind may be running a mile a minute, but if you stay grounded inside your body, your mind will slow down."

Nate: hello?

Kayleigh: sorry, I'm here.

Nate: so u w2m l8r?

Kayleigh: k, whr?

Nate: my house

Kayleigh paused and gulped in air. Anne put her hands out flat, palms down, and made motions that must have meant "calm down." Kayleigh opened her mouth wide and sucked in air until it filled her lungs. She had never been to Nate's house before, and already anxiety clawed at her midsection. She accepted the panic and searched for information that she may or may not need to act upon, and placed her thumbs on her phone.

Kayleigh: k, when?

Nate: how bout after lunch? 38 Clover Drive

Kayleigh: k, c u then.

Nate: gr8!

Kayleigh let out the breath she'd been holding as she had texted. "Ugh. I told him I'd go over to his house after lunch." She looked at Anne, the corner of her lip scrunched into a grimace, and hoped Anne might talk her out of it.

"That sounds like fun." Anne placed a plate of sandwiches in front of Kayleigh. "Take a few days to learn mindfulness, use it in everyday interactions, and then we'll move on to the second lesson."

Kayleigh picked up a ham and cheese on white and took a bite, trying to be mindful of the salty ham, sweet cheese, and fluffy bread. "How many lessons are there again?"

"There are three main principles of morphing that allow you to manage your mind, body, and soul. There are as many lessons as you need to master these principles. The first, mindfulness, we practiced today. When you're ready, we'll move on to working with your body."

"The body? Oh, great."

"It'll be fine." Her teacher chuckled.

Kayleigh nodded and washed down her sandwich with some iced tea.

Anne passed her a napkin and winked. "Now, go hang out with your male friend."

Kayleigh finished her lunch and said goodbye to Anne, who morphed back into Mrs. O'Neill in the safety of the hallway before opening the door. Kayleigh marveled at how smoothly Anne moved between two distinct forms. In seconds, she changed from one person to another.

As Kayleigh walked along the damp sidewalk, the rich, pungent smell of moist earth hung heavy in her nostrils. Several brave crocus buds in sunny yellow and light purple poked their heads through the ground in the bare beds that lined the streets.

She unzipped her jacket, so relieved spring had arrived, and let the playful breeze dance over the skin of her neck. Her father was teaching an intensive weeklong seminar this week, so he trusted her to stay out of trouble during the day and be home for dinner.

The sun warmed her face, and a gust of wind pushed her bangs off her forehead. She paused and closed her eyes, mindful of the chirping birds in the trees, the rustle of the wind through the leaves, and the water dripping off the branches onto the pavement.

A loud *caw* broke her concentration, and her eyes popped open. A black bird, larger than a crow, sat nearby on a wooden fence that ran the length of Nate's side yard. The sun glinted off its wings in shades of deep blue and rich purple. The raven's thick beak curved at the tip, and it vocalized again, a deep throaty sound that sailed over the wind.

Kayleigh reached the front of Nate's yard and turned to look back at the bird. The raven unfolded its wings, pushed off with its feet, and sailed towards Kayleigh. She put out one arm and marveled at the size of the bird's wingspan. It seemed as big as her arm. Suddenly, she realized the bird was headed straight for her.

She ducked and caught a flash of gray out of the corner of her eye. A large dog jumped past her towards the bird, brushing her arm. She fell to the pavement and watched as the bird twisted in midair to avoid the dog and flapped up to land on a bare tree across the street.

Kayleigh studied the dog, which reminded her of an Alaskan malamute or a sled dog, only much leaner and scruffier. It crossed the street and bared its teeth at the raven. A low growl rumbled from behind its sharp canines.

Kayleigh scrambled to get up, wondering from which yard the dog had escaped. She unlocked Nate's gate quickly and shut it behind her. When she turned back towards the street, she didn't see either the raven or the dog. Bare oaks and maples lined the sidewalk, and the sun glinted off the puddles that dotted the road.

Her heart beat like a bass drum in her ears from the wild kingdom encounter, and she scanned the yard for any other rabid animals. She brushed the dirt off the bottom of her pants and took several breaths, preparing herself to meet Nate. A porch wrapped around the house on three sides, and the wood creaked under her feet as she approached the door. She took several breaths to steady herself and pressed Nate's doorbell.

She tried to be mindful rather than afraid of the tight feeling in her chest and the nerves that clamored at her to run and hide. She no longer wanted anxiety to keep her from something — or someone — she wanted, so she willed herself to observe the panic, but not react to it.

The object of her desire opened the door, and her breath caught in her throat. Nate had dressed in a red and white striped shirt under a blue hoodie. His faded jeans, worn and ripped on both knees, hung slightly off his hips and tapered down his legs to hug his ankles.

"Hi." Kayleigh's voice didn't waver, and she surprised herself by sounding calm despite the turmoil that twisted and writhed in her gut. There was no reason for her to be anxious or afraid. She was visiting a friend, plain and simple.

"Hey. Come on in." Nate stepped back and took her coat.

Kayleigh's eyes widened as she gazed at the high ceiling of the entranceway and the broad wooden stairs that led to the second floor. Nate's house was also on the town's historic registry.

She followed him into the family room, where a large television had been paused in the middle of a video game, something with elves and coins. He turned crimson and hastened to turn it off.

"That's not that interesting. There's just not much to do this week. I usually go camping during spring break, but with all the extra snow melting this season, there were reports of mudslides in the Catskills, and we decided to stay home."

"It seems too cold for camping."

"I like to camp all year round, actually. I have gear for all types of weather. Keeps me warm."

"Be prepared. The Boy Scout motto, right?" Kayleigh asked.

"Yeah. Or in the winter, we'll stay in a cabin and keep a fire going."

Kayleigh thought about snuggling in front of a fire with Nate, and she blushed. She looked at him, and he appeared bright pink as well. She longed to brush the strands of pale hair off his forehead and count the flakes of green in his blue eyes. A whole new kind of warmth crept over her body, one she hadn't been aware existed beneath the fear. Her stomach did somersaults, and a tingle tiptoed down her torso.

"Please, have a seat. I'll get us some drinks." He disappeared into the kitchen, and Kayleigh sank into the large sofa.

Beep beep.

She fished her phone out of her bag without thinking and unlocked the screen. The black circle jumped out at her, and her pulse quickened.

Anonymous: Afternoon booty call?

Kayleigh flushed as if she'd stepped into a sauna fully clothed, and her eyes immediately flew to the window. Someone knew she was at Nate's.

Her heart threatened to pound out of her chest, and her pulse throbbed in her temple. She surveyed the back yard, frantically searching for signs of someone lurking with binoculars.

She focused on Nate's lacrosse net set up on the grass and willed herself to be mindful. A simple text should not have the power to reduce her to a trembling mouse.

Kayleigh stood in the family room and tried to keep her breathing slow and even. She remembered what Anne had said about being grounded so she could experience everything happening in her body and deal with her emotions. Grounded, as in connected to the earth, solid and focused, not floating around like a heart-shaped balloon on Valentine's Day. Like trees. Trees were grounded. She could be a tree.

Kayleigh's legs grew heavy, and her skin thickened into bark. Her phone dropped from her hands and clattered on the floor. Her fingers stretched into wooden limbs, twisted roots snaking from the tips towards the floor, pulling her off the stool. The telltale shimmer of morphing traveled up her body as her torso lengthened and changed into a trunk. A clump of leaves burst from Kayleigh's hair as it darkened into forest green, and willow branches replaced her auburn strands.

Kayleigh tilted her head towards her body and several boughs flopped over her shoulder, laden with long foliage. She tried to move her feet, but they resided as solidly on the floor as the wooden legs of a rustic table.

Fright overran her body, and her mind blanked. She was a tree. Right in front of the window. This could not be happening. This was the first time she'd changed her entire body into something else, and she wasn't sure how to get back to being herself.

Be Kayleigh. Be me.

She tried to say her name out loud, but the rough bark on her lips cracked as she opened her mouth. She could only wheeze, which rustled the leaves that draped over where her arms should have been. The refrigerator closed in the kitchen and a clink of glasses signaled Nate's approach. He would walk in here any minute and find a new houseplant. One wearing Kayleigh's clothes.

I am not a weeping willow. I am Katherine Leigh Paz-Purcell, a fifteen-year-old girl.

The bark smoothed back into skin, and the shrubbery on her head flattened into hair. The wood in her limbs lightened into muscle, and the bark became skin and clothing again.

Kayleigh let out a long sigh and licked her lips. No bark, just skin.

The door swung open, and Nate walked in carrying drinks. He set the glasses on the coffee table and looked at Kayleigh. "I poured us some soda…what happened to you?"

She brushed the hair out of her face and plastered a smile on her face. Her knees wobbled.

"You look a bit green. Are you feeling okay?" He placed a hand on her forehead and examined her face.

"I'm just a little…"

"Sit down before you keel over." He placed a hand under her elbow and guided her to the sofa. "We don't need you fainting again."

Great, he remembered her timber act in the cafeteria.

He sat and pulled her down next to him, putting an arm around her shoulders. Her head dropped onto his chest, and his other hand found hers. She closed her eyes and breathed in the scent of laundry soap and body wash. Heavenly.

Beep beep.

Kayleigh groaned and glanced to where she had dropped her phone on the floor. "It's just a text."

"Don't you want to know who sent it?" Nate asked.

She didn't want to leave the warmth of his arms, but she leveraged herself off the couch and scooped her phone from the floor. Anger boiled her blood as she read the next text from her anonymous tormentor.

Anonymous: Stealing Hannah's boyfriend?

Kayleigh scoffed, refusing to let words send her into a panic anymore. Whoever was spying on her clearly wasn't going to physically approach her at this point, and all the person could do was throw words at her. She snorted, sat back on the sofa, and handed the phone to Nate. "Go ahead and read them."

As he read the texts from the anonymous black circle, his face reddened, and his jaw tensed. He chewed his lip, and his free hand formed a fist at his side. Kayleigh thought back to the first text about her mother, the one about Odette dying, and remembered the Nonys that had made her faint in the cafeteria and run from Emma. She noticed some pangs of worry pinch her chest, but she wasn't going to let emotions run her over anymore.

She smiled. *Thanks, Anne.*

"Who wrote these?" Nate asked. He clenched his teeth together, and there was a hard edge to his voice.

"I originally thought Emma wrote all of them, including the Nonys to go along with her mean comments on Me3, but the last time she bullied me in the hallway, she seemed surprised that someone else had sent something nasty my way."

"It's true that she didn't ever try to hide her treatment of you," Nate said. "She didn't care if what she said made her racist and mean."

"Is it true?"

"That she's a horribly misguided person? Absolutely."

Kayleigh paused, the doubt still hanging over her head like a storm cloud. It was time to take a risk. "I mean the part about stealing you from Hannah." She placed a hand on his forearm and looked up at him from beneath her lashes.

He exhaled and shifted slightly in his seat. "I was never hers to begin with." He hesitated and covered her hand with his. "It's always been you." He leaned forward until she could see the ocean in his eyes.

Kayleigh closed the distance between them and placed her lips firmly on his. A jolt of excitement ignited within her, and she held the soft kiss for several seconds. She leaned back and smiled at Nate, whose azure eyes widened.

Nate moved closer and claimed her lips, his eyes fluttering closed. She allowed her mouth to part slightly, and his roamed over hers with a gentle pressure that made her heart thud against her ribcage. A small moan escaped from his throat.

A delicious tingle grew in her belly and spread downwards, surprising her. New sensations of arousal flooded her body, both exhilarating and slightly scary. His hand slipped around her waist, and she gasped, pulling away with a giggle. She'd gone too far into unfamiliar territory.

Nate cleared his throat and shifted on the couch, tugging on one pant leg. Kayleigh could only grin at him and hope she didn't look too flushed—her whole body seemed feverish. He returned the smile, his face beaming.

"So want to be an elf?" He gestured to the game console where the case for "Magical Forest 3" lay on top.

Kayleigh nodded, and for the rest of the afternoon she let Nate guide her through a land of elves, trolls, and faeries.

Mindfulness had led to courage, and she couldn't wait for the next round of Anne's training.

CHAPTER ELEVEN

BODY

A couple of days later, the urge to learn more about morphing drew Kayleigh back to her teacher. Anne welcomed her with a smile and fed her breakfast as they made small talk. Kayleigh wasn't sure she could say she had mastered mindfulness because turning into a tree probably didn't count as being grounded. She wanted to wait for the right time to tell Anne she had literally grown roots.

"It seems like we're in luck," Anne said, pulling open the sliding door. A warm breeze lifted the hair off Kayleigh's forehead and blew out the sandalwood candle on the mantle. "It's warm enough for us to have our lesson outside."

The garden showed signs of spring. Crocuses lined the beds of trees that had sprouted little tufts of new leaves. Several tall fruit trees also showed evidence of new growth. Anne took a damp towel and wiped off the iron patio set occupying the center of the lawn. She set a tray with tea and scones on the table, sat, and adjusted her tennis shoes. Kayleigh sat across from her.

"The second principle of morphing actually involves two related concepts: proprioception and the vestibular system," Anne said.

"Proprio—what?" Kayleigh asked.

Anne chuckled and turned her face to the sun. She closed her eyes, tilted her head back, and sighed. "Proprioception. That's our inner sense of the location of parts of our bodies and how we coordinate and move our limbs." With her eyes still closed, she stretched out one arm, pointed her index finger, and then brought it in to touch her nose.

"Ah, I get it," Kayleigh said.

Anne opened her eyes and continued. "Our vestibular system is responsible for balance and spatial orientation. As we move, the body knows how to control our eye movements and our muscles to keep us upright."

She stood and raised her arms over her head, placing her hands palms together. She lifted one foot and placed the sole on the opposite inner thigh, toes down. Kayleigh could see her muscles tremble slightly to keep her balance.

"This is a yoga move called *Vrksasana* or the tree." After a few moments Anne slowly lowered her foot and arms. "Are you familiar with yoga?"

"I'm familiar with trees," Kayleigh said. Her cheeks ignited with the heat of a summer sun, and she pretended to study the moss growing between the flagstones under the patio set.

Kayleigh snuck a glance at Anne, who tipped her head to one side and furrowed her brows as she returned to the table and sat down. She poured a cup of tea and paused before taking a sip, her eyes roaming over Kayleigh's face.

"Okay, I accidentally turned myself into a sapling three days ago. Sorry." Kayleigh blurted it, caving under Anne's scrutiny. "I was trying to think about being grounded, like you said, and then that led to thinking about trees, and suddenly I was a weeping willow."

"Let's not use any imagery for now. That will come with step three."

"Sorry," Kayleigh repeated. She picked up a scone and nibbled at its tip.

"For now you still need to practice mindfulness and today's concept of body awareness," Anne said. "I want you to take note of everything that your mind and body are doing, but observe with the cool detachment of a sociologist studying the modern culture of teenagers. Fascinating but not alarming."

"Pretend I'm studying myself?"

"In a way...yes. Not your behavior, per se, but your inner experience. Rather than reacting immediately to every sensation or emotion, you're going to observe it, pause, and regulate it a bit by letting the strongest ones go. Don't try to escape from the feelings with any particular image."

"And for now, I'll stay away from picturing any plants, animals...or balloons."

Anne grinned. "Correct. Tell your brain to stay present in your body, your *human* body. Then, your mind won't wander off and take over."

"Got it." Kayleigh relaxed into the chair and took a bite of pastry.

Anne set down her teacup and walked to a flat patch of grass several feet away. "Kinesthetic awareness is another name for the external sense of our body in space and time. In other words, it's our knowledge of our form in relation to the immediate environment. We use it to throw a baseball or to dance."

Anne stood with her feet shoulder-width apart and her hands at her sides. She brought one hand up as she shifted her weight to the side and bent her knee.

"Tai chi, right?" Kayleigh asked.

Anne nodded. For the next several moments her hands floated from one position to another, the movements fluid yet precise. After twenty-four poses, she returned to her starting position.

"You did that beautifully," Kayleigh said.

"Now you," Anne said.

"Oh, I don't know. I'm not the most graceful person."

"Come on." Anne tugged on Kayleigh's arm and pulled her off the chair. "It is important for all people of every age to move their bodies. Challenge your vestibular system and fine tune your proprioception." She dragged Kayleigh to the patch of grass and posed her like a mannequin in the first tai chi position.

"I feel silly." Kayleigh let her rib cage sag and blew a raspberry through her lips.

"Think of it this way." She pushed Kayleigh's shoulders back up and stood next to her. She moved into the next position and glared at Kayleigh until she followed. "In order to be a better morph, you don't only need to practice honing your senses. Morphs don't only have five—sight, hearing, taste, smell, and touch—but we develop a sixth and seventh sense. Basically, you master what your body is doing on the inside and what your body is doing on the outside."

Kayleigh followed half-heartedly and wished Anne would get straight to the morphing. All the eastern Buddhist mindfulness and lessons on the central nervous system were taxing her brain.

A blur of movement and color startled her. Anne's form shifted in seconds, her golden curls transforming to patches of black and white, which spread down her neck and shoulders. Her body dropped over on all fours as her limbs thickened and became fuzzy. The bridge of her nose, now covered in white hairs, lengthened and grew a dark leathery snout, round ears traveled to the top of her head, and black circles of fur surrounded her eyes. Kayleigh took several steps back and bumped into the table as the giant panda lumbered towards her.

The back of Kayleigh's legs slammed into the front of the chair, and her bottom landed in the seat with a plop. Awe overcame her, and she instinctively touched the bear that stood at least three feet tall at the shoulder.

The panda nudged her hand with the top of its head, and its soft fur tickled Kayleigh's palm. She stroked the top of one ear and marveled at how it swiveled under her touch.

After several seconds, the fur shifted under her hand and the strands clumped together into feathers. The bear's shape lengthened and unfolded into a long-necked crane, a crown of red contrasted with stark white plumage. It spread its wings and took flight, soaring over Kayleigh's head. She watched it sail into the sky, glide on the wind, and then circle back around to the garden.

As it landed on the patio, its shape blended and blurred once more, and snowy wings morphed into the draped robes of an elderly man. His elongated eyes peeked out from underneath bushy eyebrows that sat on a wrinkled face. Matching tufts of silver hair formed a mustache and long beard. He clasped his palms together and bowed at Kayleigh.

Kayleigh jumped up and stared at the old man, who continued to gaze at her with a tiny smile on his pale lips. She hesitated to touch him. He moved closer and offered her a hand.

His fingers felt tough and leathery beneath hers. Kayleigh stepped close and examined his jet black eyes. She searched for signs of Anne but saw none. Kayleigh glanced down at the man's silk pants and wondered if morphing into the other gender changed *all* body parts. She quickly dropped his hand and took a step back, embarrassed where her thoughts had taken her.

He stepped back and with a swish of his robes, morphed back into Anne. Her ivory skin and youthful face came into focus, dressed again in her cardigan and slacks. She twirled her curls around her finger and smoothed them into place. She adjusted her sweater and smoothed the material covering her thighs.

"How did you do that?" Kayleigh asked, open-mouthed.

"Practice." Anne grinned and poured herself another cup of lavender Earl Grey.

"What happens to your clothes when you morph?" Kayleigh asked. "When I turned myself into a tree, I was still wearing my clothes."

"I ripped countless outfits before I learned to slide them into a corner of the morph, out of the way." Anne chuckled and sipped at her tea. "Of course, I often ended up with my clothes on backwards coming out of a morph as well."

Kayleigh's mouth dropped open again, and she gasped. "Did you ever end up naked?"

"No, that was your mother. She thought it'd save time to canter into town as a horse, but when she got there and morphed back into human form, only pieces of torn clothing remained. She snuck around the backs of buildings, trying to find clothing drying on a clothesline. Eventually she had to abandon her plans and gallop home, sneaking into the house for more clothes." Anne smiled, and her shoulders shook with giggles. "Órla stashed extra clothes all around town because she had trouble mastering how to morph around them."

"And what about your voice? How is it you sound older when you are Mrs. O'Neill?"

"That's also an advanced skill. If you lengthen the vocal chords it changes the pitch of your voice. This skill your mum did very well—she could even change accents and add in slang. You wouldn't have any idea it was her."

"And what about the shimmer? I can see the sheen to my skin when I start to morph, and the fern I bumped into the day Mom disappeared had a shiny edge and uneven shadows."

"Aren't you twenty questions today?" Anne sighed and put down her cup. "Morphing expends much energy, some of which escapes as heat and light. Some morphs have more trouble controlling this, so they look shiny. Morphing is equal parts technical skill and magic. It comes more naturally to some morphs than others."

"Oh," Kayleigh said, wishing she had known about morphing on the day she'd slammed into the plant. Maybe she could have saved her mother.

"Okay, show time's over." Anne rose and stretched. She assumed the first position of their tai chi form and waited until Kayleigh followed.

For the rest of the morning Kayleigh practiced the ancient art of tai chi with Anne, practicing her movement, finding balance, and learning to control her body.

She obediently followed her new teacher, but doubted how an ancient form of Chinese exercise would make her a better morph or help her find her mother.

After a brief thaw, spring rains had set in and drenched the earth. Kayleigh sat at her writing desk by the window, watching the robins peck for food, their orange breasts bright against the gray drizzle. Buds had appeared on the trees, daffodils and pansies brightened the flowerbeds, and several baby bunnies ventured into the lawn with their mother.

Kayleigh had practiced mindfulness and body awareness with Anne for several weeks, but they hadn't started actually morphing. Anne said that Kayleigh wasn't ready, but wouldn't offer specifics.

Kayleigh hadn't spoken much to Bridget since they'd argued in the girls' restroom. They still had classes together and still sat at the same table for lunch, but Bridget had barely said two words to Kayleigh. Daiyu had asked Kayleigh if everything was okay, and she'd nodded. In reality, Kayleigh suspected that something else was going on with Bridget, but she couldn't put her finger on what.

On the other hand, she and Nate had grown close. They hung out most days after school when she wasn't with Anne and either talked, snuggled, or watched television. His parents and younger brother were warm and welcoming, and her father seemed to like Nate. She enjoyed the mix of security and calm that settled over her in Nate's presence, combined with a flush of excitement.

The doorbell rang, and Kayleigh glanced at the clock. Natalie was right on time. Kayleigh had asked her to come by so they could figure out who had been sending the nasty texts and Nonys all year. Time to fight back. Kayleigh hopped down the stairs two at a time and opened the front door.

"Hi," Natalie said, stepping inside and shaking the rain off her jacket.

"Hey. Thanks for coming over."

"Sure thing. I brought my gear." Natalie opened her backpack and revealed two laptops, a tablet, and some kind of silver drive. "Where should we set up?"

"In my dad's study. He's giving some Saturday series presentation at the college today, so we can use his PC if we need to." She led the way through the living room and dining room. Images of upended furniture, broken plates, and shattered picture frames flashed in her head. The only evidence of the house having been trashed existed in her mind, and it sat on her heart with a dull ache. She paused when she got to the sunroom. Over the past few years, her father had replaced all the plants that had been destroyed, including her mother's lavender and other herbs. Pots of tulips and irises enjoyed the sun streaming through the windows and waited to be transplanted outside.

The memory of the shimmering plant invaded her mind as they rounded the corner to her father's study. Kayleigh remembered being knocked to the floor and thinking that had caused her blurry vision. If she'd only known it was a morph, she might have—truth was she might be gone as well. Like her mother. Kayleigh rubbed a hand across her rib cage, acid rising from her stomach.

She took several deep breaths to calm her overactive nervous system, and she practiced mindfulness. She didn't need to be afraid of the fear, and she didn't have to morph to escape anger's wrath. She could *experience* all of those emotions—most of all regret—and not have to *become* those feelings.

Kayleigh opened the door to her father's study and surveyed the mahogany desk, behind which she'd found her father on the floor, bloody and bruised. She shook her head to rid herself of that image, focusing instead on the books that lined the walls and the musty smell of paper and leather.

"Are you okay?" Natalie asked.

"Yeah, let's get set up here." Kayleigh pulled out her father's chair, a tall-backed leather executive on wheels and motioned for Natalie to sit down. A small wooden chair sat near, but restlessness plagued her legs and she decided to stand. Emilio padded into the study and wound himself around her legs, purring.

"I'm going to hack into Nony's network," Natalie said. "See if I can trace the origin of the messages from the cafeteria and the hallway." She powered up the laptops and the PC. "It'll take a bit of time, as Nony is designed so people can remain anonymous."

Kayleigh watched as Natalie pulled more cords from her bag and connected her father's computer to her laptops. She hooked the three screens into one large desktop and then opened a small window at the bottom left corner. She typed in lines of code, and boxes of computer language popped up as she worked. One of her tablets sat on the desk, open to Emma's Me3 page, which showed a picture of Kayleigh the zombie.

Natalie's chocolate brown eyes focused intently on the screens as her fingers clicked away on the keyboards. Kayleigh envied Natalie's olive skin and the way her coffee-colored waves brushed her shoulders. Kayleigh twisted her copper locks into a knot and reminded herself to accept and love all parts without judgment.

"Crud, I think I'm stuck," Natalie said. "I can see various strings of Nonys, and I've identified several key players." She pointed to the screen and a number of several digits. "See here, I can trace messages from this person back to Emma."

"Are those from the cafeteria?" Kayleigh asked.

"Well, that's the strange thing." Natalie wrinkled her forehead and her eyes bore into the screen. "Emma's pretty unoriginal. She jumps onto random conversations, and even pasted a link to her Me3 page."

"Taking the Nony out of anonymous."

"Exactly…although she could be using one of her father's accounts. When I trace the Nonys sent from the cafeteria, the account bounces through several different countries, and I'm having trouble finding the source."

"So what else can you do?" Kayleigh asked.

"Get help." Natalie grinned and pulled out her other tablet.

"What are you doing?" Kayleigh asked.

"Getting info from a friend."

"Is that safe?" Kayleigh disliked the idea of involving more people than necessary.

"It's a secure chatroom." Natalie continued typing.

T1R4M1SU: need help

"Tiramisu?" Kayleigh asked, and giggled. "That's your hacker name?"

"I'm Italian," Natalie shrugged. "And it's my favorite dessert."

Kayleigh put up her hands. "Absolutely no judgment here. My hacker name would probably be 'clueless.'"

Sh4d0w Pr0xy: wazup?

T1R4M1SU: need help with nony

Sh4d0w Pr0xy: what kind?

T1R4M1SU: look at this

With a couple of keystrokes, Natalie allowed the user to survey her work so far. Kayleigh's eyes widened as an invisible hand took over Natalie's mouse, opened several text boxes, and picked up the trail where Natalie had left off.

"Natalie, you let the guy into your computer?" Kayleigh crossed her arms over her breasts and grimaced.

"It's fine. Shadow Proxy and I go way back," Natalie said.

"Have you ever met him in real life?"

"No, but I know his work. He's a white hat. An ethical hacker."

"Or so he says." A shiver ran over her shoulders and goose bumps appeared on her arms. The Internet seemed like a dark rabbit hole where bullies, stalkers, and hackers planned evil deeds.

Sh4d0w Pr0xy: user can send Nonys from anywhere, but I found where the nony account was first set up

T1R4M1SU: awesome!

Sh4d0w Pr0xy: I sent you the IP address, but it looks like a public coffee shop in Syracuse, NY.

T1R4M1SU: we'll check it out. no info on user?

Sh4d0w Pr0xy: the person logs in from shop, looks like saturdays

T1R4M1SU: any name?

Sh4d0w Pr0xy: nope, but the avatar on the account is a black circle

Kayleigh gasped. A black circle—the same symbol that had appeared next to the texts. So the person sending threats via text and via Nony was the same. Two different ways, both mobile, to threaten her. It was a lucky break that the person had registered the account from the coffee shop.

T1R4M1SU: good work, thanks

Sh4d0w Pr0xy: "Everything goes somewhere, and I go everywhere."

T1R4M1SU: LOL

Natalie signed off and turned off the computers. She rocked back and placed her hands behind her head. She grinned.

"Nice work, now pack your things, and let's go," Kayleigh said.

"We're not going to the coffee shop, are we?" Natalie's brown eyes widened.

"Why not? Shadow Proxy says the bully logs in on Saturdays. It's only about ten minutes away by bus. It's on the edge of the city close to the community college."

"You want to stalk your stalker?"

"I'm tired of being a victim. If it's Emma, I want to know."

Natalie packed up her things while Kayleigh grabbed their jackets. It had stopped raining outside, but Kayleigh grabbed an umbrella just in case.

They walked to the end of the street and stopped at the bus stop to wait for the red line, which looped around Kayleigh's neighborhood, passed Main Street, and ended up downtown near the community college.

As they waited for the bus, laughter from up the street caught Kayleigh's attention. Nate and Martin, dressed in athletic shorts and T-shirts, joked and pushed each other as they walked. Martin bounced a basketball and pretended to shoot hoops. The butterflies that had taken up residence in Kayleigh's belly started dancing a jig when she saw Nate. His eyebrows raised with surprise, and his face lit up when he caught sight of her, and he jogged the rest of the way over.

"Hey, funny seeing you here," Nate said. He leaned over and gave her a hug, lightly brushing his lips across her temple. Her heart skipped a beat and thumped out Morse code against her ribs.

"Hey, girls, you waiting for the bus?" Martin asked.

"Yes—" Natalie said.

"No—" Kayleigh said at the same time.

"Well, which is it?" Nate asked.

"And why do the two of you look so guilty?" Martin asked. His eyes narrowed until one closed.

"There's no reason. We're just going on a little stake out," Natalie said.

"It's not a stake out," Kayleigh said. "I just want to find out who is bullying me."

"Besides Emma?" Nate asked.

"That's what I want to find out," Kayleigh said.

"So we're hopping a bus to the coffee shop that apparently the bully frequents on Saturdays," Natalie said.

"And what do you plan to do when you get there?" Nate asked.

"Well, I'm not sure." Kayleigh frowned and twisted the corner of her jacket.

"I'm in," Martin said. He threw the ball up and pretended to make a basket. "Swish."

Kayleigh's head snapped up, and she stared at Martin as if he'd just grown two heads.

"What?"

"Why not?" Martin asked. "I'm up for a bus ride."

"It's a field trip," Nate said. He threw an arm around her and squeezed as the bus pulled to a stop.

Once settled, Kayleigh filled in Nate and Martin on the details that she and Natalie had uncovered. They switched buses on Main Street and got off in front of the Emerald City Cyber Café. Through large front windows, Kayleigh could see a row of computers lining a coffee bar and disappearing into the body of the restaurant. A vein in Kayleigh's neck throbbed, and she itched to confront her bully.

"Wait," Natalie said. "We can't just walk in. We should hide somewhere and spy or something."

"There's a burger place across the street," Martin said. "I could go for a bacon cheddar."

"Natalie, what do you need to locate the person?" Kayleigh asked.

"After I take a look at their system, we have to wait to see if the black circle logs in."

"Can you do that remotely?" Nate asked. Kayleigh caught the edge of excitement in his voice. He seemed to be getting into the whole cloak and dagger thing.

"I can." Natalie grinned back at him.

Kayleigh asked for a table by the window and scanned the café across the street. They were close to the college, so she saw several students with backpacks enter to get coffee and use the Internet. There was a big sign that offered free Internet for laptops and reduced rates for students to use the computers. The place seemed busy.

The waitress brought their burgers, and Kayleigh asked for water. Her tongue seemed to be coated in sandpaper, which rubbed the top of her mouth raw. She glanced often at the cyber café, barely tasting her favorite maple onion jam.

"And look who the winner is," Martin said and pointed towards the end of the street. Emma and an older male, presumably her older brother based on his similar coloring and features, walked down the lane and entered the café.

"Maybe," Natalie said. "Let's see if she logs in."

Minutes passed and Kayleigh eyed her phone, waiting for a nasty message to beep at her. Natalie watched her screen and read the numbers of the people logging in and out from the café's Internet.

Time seemed to stand still, and nothing happened. Finally, Emma and her brother left the coffee shop, carrying a paper cup.

"That doesn't prove she isn't the black circle," Natalie said. "Maybe she was too busy to be mean today."

"Look, she updated her Me3 page," Martin said. He turned his phone around and showed her page, which had a new peep.

P: college guys are so much hotter

Kayleigh stared at it, confused. Emma didn't log in as the black circle, but updated her social media?

"Still doesn't prove she isn't the black circle," Natalie said again. "She could have been more concerned about impressing guys than bullying girls today."

Kayleigh sat in silence, wondering how long they would wait. The person could have come and gone hours before they'd even arrived. She stared down at the last bite of burger.

"Uh, Kayleigh, isn't that your dad?" Nate asked.

Kayleigh watched as her father entered the coffee shop. "He must have just finished the seminar. The college is within walking distance. And he said that Emma's brother was one of his students." Her father exited a moment later, holding a small cup of coffee.

"I'm sorry we didn't find the bully," Natalie said.

"Ugh, it's so frustrating." Kayleigh balled up her napkin and tossed it on the empty plate. "It was stupid of me to think we'd show up and easily find the bully."

"It was worth a try," Nate said. He covered Kayleigh's hand with his own.

"You could always just block the bully," Natalie said. "Set the controls so you don't receive anything from that person across all social media."

"It's an option." Kayleigh shrugged. "But they could just open another account. Besides, I still have to deal with Emma."

"Whatever you need, baby girl, let us know." Martin placed his hand over Nate's and Kayleigh's.

"Me too." Natalie added her hand to the pile. "Another hack, another stake out, whatever."

"Well, we should go," Kayleigh said. She slid her hand out and fished for her wallet. She placed several bills on the table and stood. "If my father's headed back home, he'll wonder where I am."

Kayleigh put on her jacket and slowly exhaled, emptying her lungs of air. Using mindfulness to accept such disappointment seemed as insurmountable as climbing Mount Everest. She led the group out the door, but stopped short before the exit.

"What happened?" Natalie said, and plowed into Kayleigh's back.

"Look." Kayleigh pointed to the front of the café. The four of them squeezed into the vestibule to look out of the small window in the door.

Across the street, Bridget had just come out. She pulled her blue-black curls out of the back of her pea coat and buttoned it up the front. She adjusted the messenger bag on her shoulder and took a sip from a paper cup.

Kayleigh sagged against the door and leaned her forehead against the glass. She coughed, her lungs working like a balloon after the party had ended, deflated and useless.

"Is that Bridget?" Nate asked. He scooted foreword and slipped a hand around Kayleigh's waist. She turned and buried her head in his chest.

"That doesn't prove..." Natalie trailed off and placed a hand on Kayleigh's back. "She didn't log on, either."

"Bridget's gone," Martin said. "Let's go."

Kayleigh kept her head on Nate's shoulder during the bus ride home. A fog muddied her brain and lead weighted down her limbs. The tiny part of her mind that was still rational knew that between the people who showed up at the coffee shop—Emma, her father, and Bridget—Emma was the one proven bully. Of course it was a coincidence that her father had been there. He must have stopped by for a coffee after his lecture, but she couldn't explain Bridget's presence.

Natalie and Martin sat in front, whispering to each other and stealing glances at Kayleigh. She understood the word "Bridget" every so often, but she couldn't process the typhoon of questions in her head. The word frenemy had been invented for a reason, but Kayleigh refused to change Bridget from the category of best friend, no matter how strained their relationship had been lately.

Nate planted soft kisses on her head and whispered encouraging words, but no amount of mindfulness or comfort would chase away the gaping black hole in her gut.

CHAPTER TWELVE

SOUL

"You're awfully quiet this morning, *princesita*," her father said. He poured a bowl of cereal and sat across from her at the kitchen table.

"I guess," Kayleigh said. She took another bite of toast and washed it down with orange juice over ice.

"You've been spending a lot of time with Mrs. O'Neill lately," he said.

Kayleigh realized that she hadn't clued her father into the fact that Mrs. O'Neill was a morph—and her mother's cousin. It had been a busy couple of weeks, and her father had been working overtime. They'd barely seen each other, like ships passing in the night.

"Her first name is Anne," Kayleigh said.

"Isn't that a coincidence," her father said. "Your mother had a cousin, one her age, named Anne O'Neill. It's a common name in Ireland."

"A common name, yes." Kayleigh swallowed another bite of toast and cleared her throat. "But in this case it's the same Anne."

"The same Anne O'Neill?" He frowned and studied the Os floating in his bowl. "They're nowhere near the same age. The only way that's your mother's cousin would be if she's a..."

"Morph." Kayleigh finished his sentence.

"Órla's cousin…Anne. A morph." He gazed off into the direction of their neighbor's house. Emotions flashed across his face like pages flipping in a children's book. Surprise. Curiosity. Hurt.

"I'm sorry I didn't mention it before," Kayleigh said. She chuckled and tried to hide her chagrin. "You know us teens are notoriously self-centered." She aimed for casual, but ended up sounding rude, even to her ears.

"I hope you didn't mean it to be a secret, Katherine," her father said. "You've been busy frequenting burger joints with your friends."

Now it was Kayleigh's turn to look surprised. "You saw us?"

"I was actually down the street talking to a colleague when you all got off the bus," he said. "We'd finished our seminar, and I wanted to get a coffee before heading home."

"I'm sorry I didn't tell you. It was a spur of the moment trip," Kayleigh said.

"Which is why spur of the moment texting is so handy," he said. He moved his thumbs up and down in front of him, pretending to text on a phone.

Kayleigh slunk down into her hoodie and started at the ice cubes floating in her glass, bits of orange pulp clinging to their sides. In an effort to get her to drink more orange juice, her mother had always added ice and water, declaring it "special orange."

"You're fifteen now, Katherine," her father said. "I know you want to be more independent and go out with your friends. I don't want to keep you in a bubble, but you have to let me know where you're going. It can't be a secret."

Kayleigh winced at the last word. She and her father had agreed not to keep secrets. But when was the accidental omission of information a subconscious secret? She fidgeted with the swan key hanging around her neck.

"Remember how I told you about Emma, the mean girl at school?" Kayleigh asked. "Well someone has been sending me threatening texts and Nonys, and I'm not sure if it's Emma or not."

"So you stalked Emma to the cyber café?"

"Not exactly — wait, how did you know she was there?"

"Her brother, who's in my class. He came to my lecture, and I assume she tagged along."

"Oh." Kayleigh paused and wondered how much she should tell him about Bridget. It was unconfirmed information at best.

"If someone's threatening you, the police should be involved. That's far more serious than name-calling."

"Maybe, if I knew who it was." Kayleigh rubbed her eyes, the sleuthing having taken all her energy. That morning in the mirror she'd seen gray circles under her bottom lashes.

"How come you're not sure it's Emma?" he asked.

Kayleigh sat straighter and pushed the hoodie off her head. "Well, she's mean. And racist. But she's obvious about it. I think someone else has been harassing me anonymously."

"If there's social media involved, report the threatening behavior to the site's administrators, and the threats will be taken down and the person's account cancelled."

"Isn't that prohibiting freedom of speech or something?"

"Most sites have rules that prohibit offensive material and bullying. You could get them to erase anything that insulted another student."

"I hadn't thought about that." The morning sun streamed in the window and made patches of light on the table. Emilio, the tabby cat, padded into the kitchen, leapt up onto the table, and curled up in a circle of warmth. He purred, his low rumbling like a motor. Kayleigh smiled and stroked his belly.

"I think even if her meanest stuff was taken down, she'd still make comments," Kayleigh said.

"Everyone is entitled to his or her opinion," he said. "But adults have a responsibility to help teens from abusing that privilege when they veer into the realm of slander, libel, and defamation of character."

"Now, you sound like Martin's dad. Or Martin, actually, quoting his dad."

Her father finished his cereal, dropped the spoon in the bowl, and sat back. "Mr. Williams is a smart man." He glanced at his watch, got to his feet, and cleared the plates from the table. "Get to school. We'll talk more later."

Kayleigh grabbed her backpack from the mudroom, left the house, and walked to the bus stop. Her bag sat as heavy as a load of bricks on her shoulder. She shielded her eyes from the bright May sun and joined Ben and Daiyu waiting at the curb.

"Natalie told us what happened," Daiyu said. She wore a neon lemon rain jacket and held a backpack decorated with music notes. "I'm so sorry." Her black eyes studied Kayleigh. "Why didn't you tell us you'd gotten such threatening messages?"

"Aren't you on Nony?" Kayleigh asked. "Those went to everyone."

"Yeah, I saw them," Ben said. "Not funny." He tapped his foot at the edge of a puddle, sending ripples rolling along the water. The azure sky reflected in its surface blurred.

Daiyu shrugged and tucked a black strand of hair behind her ear. "My mom doesn't want me to be on so many sites. I had to beg just for a Me3 account, and she'll only let me post pictures from my dance recitals."

"That might be better," Kayleigh said. "Sometimes I don't know if social media's worth it."

"Isn't Nony an app, though?" Ben asked.

"It has to uplink to a central something-or-other, complete with GPS, in order to know where to send the messages, right?" Daiyu asked.

"I guess that's how Natalie and her hacker friend found the source," Kayleigh said.

"But Natalie said that you might have some leads on who's sending the Nonys?" Ben asked. "She wouldn't give any details."

Kayleigh made a mental note to thank Natalie for not revealing that it may be Emma or Bridget sending the messages. She wanted more time to confirm for herself before she went public with any accusations.

"Sounds like a true mystery," Ben continued. "Add up the clues, eliminate the suspects one by one." He narrowed his brown eyes and pretended to point to imaginary people. "Zero in on the culprit." He waggled his index finger at Daiyu. "I declare that it was Miss Sun, in the lunchroom, with a tablet!" He jumped melodramatically and poked her shoulder. Daiyu protested and slapped at his hand.

The bus rumbled down the street and pulled to a stop with a shriek of the brakes. The door accordioned open, squeaking on its hinges. Kayleigh got on, scanning the students for any sign of Bridget or Emma. Neither one seemed to be present, but Kayleigh's eyes met Hannah's, who looked quickly away.

Kayleigh rode the bus in silence, reviewing the lessons of mindfulness and body awareness that she and Anne had practiced. She wondered what she still had to do to prove she was ready for the third and final principle.

She plodded through the morning on autopilot, wondering why there was still no sign of Emma or Bridget. If her father had caught sight of Kayleigh getting off the bus in front of the café, then maybe Bridget had as well. That wouldn't explain why both she and Emma were not in school, however.

Kayleigh entered the cafeteria, and the noise of students talking and laughing pierced her ears like air horns at a basketball game. Martin and Nate, both dressed in lacrosse uniforms, sat with Daiyu, Ben, and Natalie.

Kayleigh slid in next to Nate and rested her head on his bicep. He threw an arm around her shoulder and continued to talk to Ben. Her friends seemed to be in the middle of a heated debate.

"Joan of Arc was only a teenager when she dressed in men's clothes and fought off the English," Nate said.

"You're wrong, Nate," Ben said. "Zenobia is clearly the better warrior. They actually called her 'the warrior queen.'"

"But Joan had God on her side," Nate said. "She had divine intervention."

"More likely seizures or schizophrenia." Ben snorted and took a bite of his roast beef.

"What are you two arguing about?" Kayleigh pulled out her peanut and jelly, still the easiest sandwich to make every morning.

"Famous female warriors," Nate said. "The history department is running the Versus Games."

"Versus Games?" Kayleigh asked.

"Theoretical battles between historical figures," Daiyu said. "It's supposed to make history fun for those that usually don't pay attention." She looked at Ben and rolled her eyes. Ben smirked and gave her a wink.

"Like Napoleon vs. Hitler, or Genghis Khan vs. Spartacus," Martin said.

"Nate and Ben got excited over the famous female warriors category and started early." It was Natalie's turn to roll her eyes.

Kayleigh raised one brow at Nate. "Female warriors?"

Nate smiled broadly and shrugged. "I already had to convince Ben that Xena the Warrior Princess wasn't an option."

"Good job," Kayleigh said. She playfully punched him on the arm.

"Isn't that sweet," Emma said behind her. "Young love."

Kayleigh groaned and turned her head to look at her pseudo-nemesis. Emma stood a few feet away, her blonde hair brushed back into a thick headband that matched her royal blue sundress.

"Still slumming, Nate?" Emma asked.

"Emma — " Nate began.

Kayleigh placed a hand on Nate's arm and gave him a nod she hoped was reassuring. She swiveled on the bench and faced Emma, looped one leg over the other, and tried to look casual.

"Yes, Emma?" Kayleigh said. The lunchroom began to quiet as Kayleigh picked up an audience. Nervousness pricked at the edge of her consciousness, and the hairs on the back of her neck stood on end. *Be mindful. I'm nervous. Anxiety is just an emotion. No need to react.*

"Kayleigh, don't you look...precious." Emma pointed to Kayleigh's faded button-down and ripped jeans. Emma turned a slow circle, inviting others to view the show.

A few giggles rose from the peanut gallery, and Kayleigh glanced at the other students. Hannah stood nearby, tugging on the edges of her sleeves until they covered her hands.

"So was this the latest special down at the thrift shop?" Emma asked. "All eyesores half off?"

Kayleigh stopped herself from shrinking back and instead rose from the bench. She placed her feet shoulder width apart and held her head high, staring directly at Emma. The cafeteria became silent.

"What bothers you, Emma? That I wear clothes?" Kayleigh asked. She held her hands out and glanced between her striped shirt and Emma's dress. "Or that I don't look like you?"

"*You* bother me, Kay*lee*. You still get special treatment years after your mother ran off. Poor *leettle* lamb." Emma imitated a Hispanic accent and whispers fluttered through the crowd.

Kayleigh's hands curled into fists and her biceps tensed. *Body awareness. Stay relaxed.* "Huh. So are you upset that something bad happened to me?"

She took a deep breath and acknowledged the tension cramping her abdomen. No need to run and hide. Emma was just a spoiled, unhappy girl. She took two steps forward, closing the distance between them.

"Or is it a problem for you that my father isn't as white as you'd like?" Kayleigh asked.

Emma opened her mouth and then paused. Vertical lines appeared between her eyebrows, and she placed one hand on her hip with a huff.

Kayleigh pressed on, Emma's silence fueling her resilience. "So help me to understand. Really, what it is that bothers you about me so much, Emma? Why do you spend time and energy putting up pictures of me on your Me3 page and making comments?"

Emma froze.

Kayleigh smiled and walked forward until she could see the strokes of blue lining Emma's bottom lashes. "I'm starting to feel flattered."

Several gasps sounded behind her. Emma's mouth dropped open, and she gaped at Kayleigh. Scarlet streaks appeared on her face, and beads of perspiration broke out on her forehead. Someone in the back started clapping.

"You're right, Kayleigh," Emma said, quickly recovering. She stepped back and surveyed the crowd. "This is a waste of time." She ran a hand over her hair and adjusted her dress. She motioned for Hannah and Madison, the other girl in her mean girl posse, to join her. They turned and walked off.

Applause and cheers erupted from the crowd. Kayleigh breathed a sigh of relief, her shoulders relaxed, and her head dropped to her chin. Nate jumped off the bench and hugged her. Martin and Ben high-fived, while Daiyu sagged forward and blew her bangs out of her eyes.

Natalie gave her a thumbs up and held her phone high. A chorus of electronic pings, cheeps, and chirps rose over the laughter.

Kayleigh unlocked her phone and saw a barrage of Nonys and texts. One even had a video link.

Epic smack down! Click here.

Way to go, Kayleigh!

Ding-dong the witch is dead.

The corners of Kayleigh's mouth spontaneously lifted and dimples formed in her cheeks. She guessed Emma wouldn't be bothering her much anymore. Her phone beeped again.

Anonymous: I won't be so easy.

Even reading the text didn't dampen her mood. The war had begun.

"It was awesome," Kayleigh told Anne. They sat in Anne's garden, surrounded by the brilliant pink flowers of the Japanese cherry trees. Squirrels darted back and forth among the perennials, searching for buried nuts. Cardinals, blue jays, and yellow finches competed for space in the birdbath, flexing their wings and splashing in the shallow water.

Kayleigh had hopped off the bus and ran straight to Anne's house. She knew her father was still at the college, and she needed to share her story.

"I could feel the nerves crawling up my legs, and I wanted to run. But I convinced myself that the emotions were no reason to panic, and I stood my ground."

"Then, you're ready for the third principle, Kayleigh." Several pink petals drifted from the tree and landed in Anne's amber curls. She wore a pleated dress of navy and forest green that reminded Kayleigh of an Irish kilt, similar to their Scottish cousin's.

"In order to easily shift your form into something else and then know how to get back to yourself, you need a strong sense of identity. Standing up to Emma solidified who you are," Anne said.

"I'm someone she can't push around any longer. She'll probably try again, but I'll be ready."

"Exactly. In order to be an effective morph, you need a firm grasp on yourself, and you have to connect your mind, body, and soul."

Anne stood and walked to a wild rose bush. She pinched off dead buds among the fluffy pink blossoms.

"After using mindfulness to accept whatever thoughts and emotions you have inside," Anne said, "then you need to be able to let them go and empty your mind."

"That sounds like meditation," Kayleigh said.

"It's similar. Meditation is related to mindfulness, and there are several dozen forms of meditation, some using guided imagery...or imagining a safe place where you feel calm and relaxed."

"Gotcha."

Anne took a seat at the wrought iron table and continued. "Morph meditation asks you to gently wipe the mind clean and find your soul," Anne said. "When you're ready to morph, see the blank slate and then clearly picture the person, animal, or object in your mind. It's not enough to see the skin or coloring of that entity. You must feel its soul."

"Feel its soul?" Kayleigh deflated. She'd come for some concrete knowledge and lessons, but instead she got some fuzzy concept about the soul.

"In many cultures, animals and objects have spirits," Anne said. "In Ireland, the ancient people worshiped the bull, horse, raven, and other animals for having mystical properties. In Scotland, it was the bear."

"Great Britain seems too far away. How can I connect with the souls of something across the ocean?" Kayleigh asked.

"The Onondaga tribes of New York were part of the Iroquois League and lived right here where we're standing." Anne closed her eyes and held out her hands, palms down.

"Can you feel the Native Americans?" Kayleigh asked.

Anne laughed and opened her eyes. "They're not ghosts. It's not that. The Native American people believed in invisible nature spirits. Spirits inhabited rivers and rocks. There were spirits of corn, beans, and squash, and all animals have different souls."

"How do I know what animal souls feel like?" Kayleigh asked.

"This is a bit more of the mystical part of morphing," Anne said. "You may be able to imitate something on the outside, but it will be a hard change to maintain if you can't feel what it's like from the inside out."

"Its soul," Kayleigh said.

"Exactly," Anne said.

"So how do I practice that?" Kayleigh asked.

"Look at those birds over there in the fountain," Anne said. "Empty your mind of your own thoughts and emotions, and imagine what it's like to be a blue jay, for example."

"Okay. Blue jays have blue and black plumage, a crest on their heads, and white underbellies."

"That is their outer appearance, yes," Anne said. "Go deeper."

"They are noisy and feisty birds, intelligent and curious. I remember one year I was doing a science project on the back porch with pieces of aluminum foil, and every time I turned around a jay had stolen a piece to play with."

"That's good. Once you identify with the soul of the bird, then empty your mind and become that bird."

Anne closed her eyes, took a deep breath, and in an instant blurred into a blue jay. She flapped to the birdbath and splashed down, flipping water over her wings and lifting her feathers into a fluffy ball.

Kayleigh laughed and watched the bird shake off the water, push from the feeder, and sail to a nearby tree. A nearby blackbird stared at the jay, gave a shriek, and flew away. The jay sailed off the tree and in a blur of color became Anne once more.

Kayleigh clapped, once again awed at seeing the transformation right before her eyes.

Anne gave a bow. "Now you."

Kayleigh closed her eyes and thought of the jay that stole pieces of her science project. In her mind she saw the blue and black light glint off its feathers, the thick skin of its feet, and its bold attitude. She imagined folding her clothes within her and allowing the bird to shift to the outside.

Her skin tingled and moved. A shiver traveled down her arms and into her fingers. Her legs lightened and lifted up underneath her as her arms stretched out and morphed into wings. She bobbed on the air, light and effortless. Her mouth migrated into her nose and hardened into a beak, while her russet hair sculpted itself into a crest with bright feathers.

With a quick flap of her wings, Kayleigh soared, the wind carrying her to the tree. She paused and looked down at Anne between the blush-colored petals of the cherry tree. Anne seemed so large…and human.

Her talons clung to the rough bark of the branch, and she surveyed the top of Anne's house, a stone Tudor style cottage. She noticed several nests tucked into the stones at the edge of the roof, and baby birds peeped their heads out and looked for their mothers.

She aimed for the bird feeder and jumped off the tree, spreading her wings and trying to catch a current of air. She careened downward and landed in the puddle on top of the stone basin. Cold water rushed around her body and startled her.

A yelp sounded in her throat, and her beak popped into a nose, becoming cartilage and flesh. Her legs became heavy, and she tumbled off the fountain onto the soft moss. As she morphed back into human form, the feathers on her arms disappeared and her flannel shirt, heavy with rainwater from the birdbath, draped over her body. Locks of wet hair plastered to her face dripped water into her eyes.

"Oops. I should have warned you about water," Anne said.

Kayleigh sat on the ground and reacquainted herself with her human form. For a moment her arms hung like useless appendages weighing her down. She used her proprioception to find her legs and position them under her body. She stood, wobbling.

"But for your first purposeful morph, not bad," Anne said. "You're a quick learner, and you have some natural skill. Let's go dry off."

A loud squawk pierced the air and silenced the twitters of the smaller birds. Kayleigh scanned the evergreens and large deciduous trees lining the outside of the fence and saw a black sheen peeping through the green. She picked out the raven's form perched among the branches.

"That's weird," Kayleigh said.

"What is?" Anne asked.

"When I was walking to Nate's house I saw a similar bird. It was just as big," Kayleigh said. She pointed to the creature. "I think it's a raven, but I didn't know they were so common in this area."

"They're not," Anne said. "They usually stay in more rural areas." Her eyes narrowed, and she studied the bird. Her eyebrows pulled together and Kayleigh read alarm on her face.

"What's wrong?"

"Let's get inside. I don't trust that anything out of the ordinary is merely a coincidence."

Kayleigh changed into some of Anne's sweats and sat in the family room, drinking a cup of water. Her mind replayed the cold of the birdbath, which had shocked her right out of the morph.

"So if you're hurt, do you automatically lose your morph?" Kayleigh asked.

"Not necessarily. It depends upon the skill of the morph," Anne said. "Those with more experience are not distracted by pain or freezing water." She laughed and ruffled Kayleigh's hair, which was still damp.

"Ha ha, make fun of the newbie."

"All things considered, you did do well your first real try. I meant it when I said you're a fast learner. I remember as soon as Órla and I found out we were morphs, we started by trying to turn ourselves into all sorts of things."

"Like what?"

Anne started giggling, her face blushing. "At first we could only get certain body parts to morph, though. Remember I told you that your mother would gallop into town as a horse? Well, the first time she tried, she only got her back end to morph into a horse. She didn't even look like a centaur. That at least would have been okay. She was only half a centaur." She grabbed her stomach as she laughed.

Kayleigh giggled and pictured two teenaged girls morphing into a variety of freak show creatures. She didn't do so badly by comparison, actually, and a wave of pride rushed over her. Confidence.

"Anne, could you excuse me a moment?"

"Sure," Anne said, still smiling.

Kayleigh went to her purse and found her phone. She pulled up the thread of texts from the anonymous bully, and for the first time since the attacks began, she hit reply:

Kayleigh: it's time we met

She held her breath and wondered if it was a good idea to directly challenge the bully. She had no idea who was at the other end of the threats, but she was tired of waiting to find out.

Anonymous: suit yourself. tonight. OHS. 8 pm.

Good idea or not, she was determined to put an end to this game.

CHAPTER THIRTEEN

BULLIES

Kayleigh ate dinner with Anne, gave her father a quick call, and then told them both she was going to meet Daiyu at the school for the science fair. So much for no more secrets. In reality, the activity had already ended, Daiyu earning a blue ribbon, but Kayleigh had asked her to wait at the school. She needed a backup plan if things went south.

Kayleigh approached the school's side emergency exit, her heart pounding in her throat. She knocked twice, hoping Daiyu would answer as planned.

The door slowly swung open. Daiyu peeked out, her dark eyes the size as quarters, her forehead streaked with worry lines.

"Thanks for staying," Kayleigh said and slunk into the hallway.

"What on earth is going on?" Daiyu asked with a strained whisper. "I told my mom I was going to your house, but in reality I've been sneaking around for twenty minutes trying to avoid the janitor."

"I know. I'm sorry." Kayleigh hugged her friend.

"Guys—"

A figure appeared down the hall, making Kayleigh yelp.

"It's Ben," Daiyu said. "Ouch, stop squeezing me."

Kayleigh relaxed her grip and stepped back, taking several deep breaths to get a grip on her nerves. "Ben?"

"I asked him to come." Daiyu raised one shoulder and tipped her head to the side. "You called me to ask that I meet you here as backup without telling me the details. You didn't think that I'd need backup, as well?" Her breathing came out in short huffs, and a pang of guilt ran through Kayleigh.

Ben approached with his red hoodie pulled up around his face, although he couldn't hide a wide grin. "The janitor is on the other side of the school by the library. What's the plan?"

"Well, I decided it's time to meet my bully, so I replied to the anonymous texts and suggested we meet."

"And you couldn't have picked a time...not in the middle of the night?" Daiyu exhaled sharply and balled her hands into fists at her sides.

"It's barely eight o'clock, Daiyu," Ben said. He waggled his eyebrows and chuckled. "I think this is fun."

Kayleigh rolled her eyes at Ben. "You two wait here. If I'm not back in thirty minutes, then call the cavalry."

Ben clasped the edge of his Timex Chronograph and pushed a button. He nodded. "Thirty minutes."

Kayleigh glanced one last time at Ben and Daiyu and tiptoed through the hallway. She paused at the music room, but only an eerie silence greeted her. The HVAC system had already shut off for the evening, leaving the air warm and stagnant. Shadows partially covered the hallways, broken only by small circles from the emergency lights.

She peeked around the corner leading to the cafeteria and carefully stepped along the hall. The science fair had let out over an hour ago, and the displays had been cleared. Kayleigh paused and entered the cafeteria, cringing at the sound of the door that clicked into place behind her. The tables, now folded in a row, cast long shadows. A forgotten foam model of the earth lay broken on the floor.

She peered in the windows to the kitchen and tried the door. Locked. She wished she had been more specific when the anonymous student had suggested meeting at the school. She made her way back to the hall and gingerly closed the cafeteria door.

Her pulse pounded in her head like someone was hitting her with a two-by-four. The tightness in her chest made it hard to breathe. *Stay calm. Be mindful. It's okay to be afraid but not to let it take you over.*

A clang in the distance came from the direction of the gymnasium. Either the janitor had made his way from the library to the gym, or it was the bully.

Kayleigh kept close to the lockers and traipsed down the hallway, glancing into empty classrooms. A lone page of math homework lay in a pool of light.

She reached the corner leading to the gym corridor. She gathered her courage and willed herself to be strong. No more running and hiding. *I will not be a victim any longer.*

She stepped around the corner and planted her feet. There, at the end of the hallway, stood Bridget. Her long hair gleamed purple in a pool of red light under an exit sign. She stood with one hip against the wall, the skirt of her dress swinging over one bent knee. She looked casual and relaxed as she flicked away imaginary dirt from under her fingernails.

"Bridget." Kayleigh took several steps towards her best friend and stopped, afraid. The wheels began to turn in her mind, and she put the pieces together. "You were the only one not there in the cafeteria that day I fainted, and you stepped into my bathroom to text me on Halloween. The day Emma cornered me in the hallway, you were there, with all the other students on their phones. You could easily have sent me those Nonys."

"What if I did send those messages?" Bridget straightened off the wall and stepped out of the red light into a shadow. Her heels clicked on the floor.

"That makes you a bully." Kayleigh told herself not to move. To stand her ground. "And not my best friend."

"Aww. Can't I be both?" Sarcasm dripped off Bridget's tongue as she moved from the shadow. She walked in a slow circle around Kayleigh.

"I don't need a frenemy, thank you." Betrayal rose like bile in Kayleigh's throat, and she swallowed to push the acid back down.

"How about a partner?" Bridget placed one hand on her hip and the other palm up.

"A partner?"

"Like an exercise partner, only instead of running, we'll be morphing." Bridget threw her hand in the air and twirled. The colors of her clothing blurred as she turned. Her skin and hair lightened, and she lost several inches. When she spun to a stop, she was the mirror image of Kayleigh.

Kayleigh gasped. "You're a morph!" Kayleigh looked at her doppelgänger, complete with freckles and frizzy auburn curls. Emotions swirled through her unchecked—shock, fear, betrayal—as if someone had hit the puree button on a blender.

"That's right," the Kayleigh clone said with Bridget's voice.

"This whole time? Who are you?"

"I'm a morph," Bridget said and shrugged. She held out her arms, and her skin shimmered and darkened into blue-black. Feathers grew out of her skin, wings dropped down from her upper arms, and her legs shriveled into black spindles with long talons. The middle of her body turned in on itself, her clothes disappeared, and she changed into a bird.

The raven squawked and flew at Kayleigh, who jumped and backed up into a locker. The metal creaked under her weight. Blue-black light glinted off its wings as they flapped, stirring the air in the hallway. Kayleigh cringed and raised her hands to protect her face.

A surge of adrenaline shocked her fight or flight mechanism, and the urge to run overwhelmed her. She slid along the lockers, desperate to get out of the flight path of the raven. *No, no more running.*

She shook her head, making the choice to stay and fight. Underneath the instinct to flee lay a more primitive force, a raw energy willing to fight. Kayleigh summoned that aggression and let it flow over her as swift as lava down the side of a volcano. She primed herself to attack.

She emptied her mind of any thought related to fear and confusion, conjuring up all the lessons that Anne had already taught her. She'd not had as much practice as she would have liked, but it was time to jump into the deep end. Sink or swim.

She thought of a blank canvas as Anne had instructed and projected her cat, Emilio, onto the white. His orange-striped coat, light green eyes, and sharp claws came into focus. She thought of how he bugged her to get food, meowed when he wanted to be petted, and ignored her when he wanted to be left alone. She imagined his soul. Persnickety and haughty.

Her body shimmered and stretched, her arms fell to the floor as paws, and her tailbone lengthened into a tail. She hissed, arched her back, and flexed her claws. She ran at the raven and leapt into the air, teeth exposed. She landed on the body of the bird and sank her nails into the raven's back.

The body of the fowl shifted and shimmered under Kayleigh's weight. Feathers gave way to fur, and the hollow bones became dense and heavy. The shape of a German shepherd, Bridget writhed and tossed Kayleigh the cat off her back. Kayleigh spun in the air, flipped right side up, and landed on her feet, back arched. The black and brown dog snarled, pulled its lips back to reveal sharp teeth, and crept towards Kayleigh, drool dripping off its incisors.

The janitor rounded the corner and stopped dead in front of the dog and cat. Kayleigh hissed at him, and the dog growled, low and menacing. The janitor clutched the collar of his dark blue overalls and backed up slowly, grabbing his phone. As soon as he cleared the corner, his feet pounded the floor, and he fled.

Kayleigh adjusted the picture in her head of the tabby cat into its larger cousin, the tiger. Her body morphed but her clothing stretched, tearing on one side. *Fold the clothes to one side, concentrate on the image, summon the magic.* With renewed energy, her muscles strained to take on the weight of the larger feline. A groan escaped her mouth as she struggled, black stripes lining her fur. She imagined the sounds the tigers made at the zoo and the groan changed to a roar that rumbled in her throat. She charged at the dog.

The canine vaulted down the hall towards Kayleigh and rammed into her. The dog knocked her over and grabbed her shoulder with its teeth. Fatigue overwhelmed her, and she started to lose the morph. Her muscles withered, and the dog's teeth pierced her skin. Sharp pain sent another rush of adrenaline through her brain.

She intensified the representation in her mind of the South China Tiger that she had seen on a calendar in the local Asian restaurant. Kayleigh remembered Daiyu explaining the animals of the Chinese Zodiac, including the tiger with its bravery, competitiveness, and love of challenges. *Brave.*

The emblem in her head deepened, and she connected with the soul of a tiger. Fearless. Passionate. Her body rippled and solidified into the fierce feline. She would not go down without giving it all she had.

Kayleigh lunged to the side, taking Bridget with her, and the two animals slammed into the door to the gymnasium. The doors swung open, and Kayleigh landed inside and rolled onto the basketball court. The blow knocked the canine's jaw loose, and Kayleigh let the animal slump to the polished wood.

Kayleigh backed up on all fours, her large paws smacking the deck. She let out a roar, which came out half howl and half scream as she morphed back into her own body. "Stop!" The sound echoed in the empty gymnasium.

She righted herself on two legs, and tufts of fur disappeared into her pores. The apricot fur on her head became hair, and stripes became freckles. Her clothing slid to the outside of her body, the top of one shoulder torn and ragged, her jeans loose. At least she wasn't naked.

The German shepherd shook, as if drying itself after a bath. As it shimmered, its back shrank and thinned into a fur coat. Bridget's body slid out from underneath, and she pushed herself back up onto two legs. Her dress slid neatly into place, and she looked as polished as she did before they'd started fighting.

Kayleigh pushed at the hair that frizzed around her face and looked down at the seam of her jeans that had ripped partially open along the leg. A rush of red-hot rage streaked along her cheekbones. She panted from the physical exertion of morphing and fighting with Bridget. "So it's true. You threatened me all along, even though you're a fellow morph."

"Is it so hard to imagine? Bullies can be anyone. Remember my father?"

"Why me?" The anger receded, and the ache of betrayal squeezed her chest. Kayleigh's eyes filled with tears, and she quickly brushed them away. "I'm your friend."

"You may have thought you were my friend, but you were only an assignment, one I was forced to take." Bridget's eyes shone like ice as she stared at Kayleigh.

"An assignment?" Kayleigh shook her head. "I don't understand."

Bridget pulled out a crumpled piece of paper from her dress pocket. She walked towards Kayleigh with strong, angry strides and thrust the paper into her hands. "Take a look!"

The piece of paper was worn at the edges and had been folded and unfolded many times. Kayleigh felt her hand shake, and she hesitantly peeled open one corner. The paper felt slightly rough and thick, like the parchment that had accompanied the key.

Her own face stared back at her. It was drawn with thin, precise lines in various colors of ink. It reminded her of the sketches the Renaissance artists did when they were studying a person for a portrait. The edges were smudged, but someone had captured a distinctly lost expression on her face.

"What is this?" she asked. Her knees buckled under her, and she sank to the floor, the wind knocked out of her sails.

"That's my assignment. You. I was put here to watch you. To see if you changed."

"Who gave you the assignment? Who sent you?"

Bridget paused and frowned, her eyes squeezing shut. She shook her head and crossed her arms across her chest. "They're an old and powerful organization. The less you know, the less of a threat you are to them." She opened her eyes, and Kayleigh saw a flash of fear.

"Did they kidnap my mother?"

"I don't know for sure."

Kayleigh's stomach twisted into a hard knot that tugged on her heart and tightened her chest. "So you knew what was happening to me all along...but you were skeptical. You didn't believe me."

"It was all an act. I couldn't reveal myself to you, so I watched you...struggle." Bridget hesitated on the last word, and her sneer softened. "You were so passive. Whine, whine. All complaining and no action."

"Why?"

"Why was I sent here?" Bridget shrugged. "I would think it would be obvious."

"Why did you terrorize me?" Kayleigh used her sixth sense and found her legs within the tornado of emotions ravaging her body. She stood, advancing on Bridget. The anger rumbled through her body, and the edge of her skin shimmered. Kayleigh backed up and took a deep breath. She accepted her emotions—anger, confusion, pain—but would not let them morph her into escape. *Stay me. Stay Kayleigh.* "Why send me nasty Nonys and try to make me feel bad about myself?"

"To toughen you up!" Bridget replied. "And clearly you needed it. You were ready to crumble the first day of high school at the first semi-mean glance from Emma. You can't be a morph and be so fragile."

"Fragile? Are you kidding me? Someone came into our home and hurt my father. My mother disappeared. While I suffered traumatic aftereffects, my body changed into a morph. And you thought I needed even more to deal with?"

Suddenly, Kayleigh remembered the assignment in her hand. She dropped it on the floor as if it had stung her and stepped back.

"Why meet me now?" Kayleigh rubbed her eyes and pulled her fingers through her hair in frustration.

"I got tired of waiting. It was exhausting pretending not to know about morphing. I'm glad you finally found the balls to confront me." She walked in a slow circle, as confident as a model on a catwalk.

Questions swirled in Kayleigh's mind. She closed her eyes and tried to use mindfulness to calm the inner storm, but she wondered what else Bridget knew about the other morphs. Footsteps vaguely registered in the whirlwind of thoughts, and she realized her frenemy had walked towards the exit.

Kayleigh's eyes popped open as Bridget opened the door, shaking her black hair off her shoulders. The edges of her frame shimmered and lifted.

"No, you can't leave without telling me more!" Kayleigh lunged towards Bridget, tackling her. The door slammed shut with a thud that bounced over the court, and they crashed to the floor.

Kayleigh landed hard on her elbow, and a flash of searing pain shot down her arm. She heard a loud grunt as Bridget hit the wood near her and yelped in pain.

The outline of Bridget's form blurred and shifted. She doubled over, grabbed her head, and rolled away from Kayleigh. Her hair shortened while her already tall frame stretched several more inches. Her shoulders broadened, and the seams on her dress stretched and partially unraveled. Her shoes popped off her feet.

Alarmed, Kayleigh slid back until she reached the wall. She cradled her left arm against her chest and watched as Bridget's body morphed into a teenaged boy. The shimmering on his skin stopped, and his body stilled. For a moment neither of them moved.

"Bridget?" Kayleigh whispered. A cold unease spread over her, and she inched farther away.

He pushed himself into a sitting position and opened his eyes. Bridget's clear blues looked back at Kayleigh from an angular male face. The resemblance was striking.

The boy scanned Kayleigh, looked around the gym, and his eyebrows drew together in confusion. He glanced down at the dress that stretched over his muscled form, and he startled, scooting back several feet on the court. Panic raced over his face, and his chest rose and fell with ragged breaths.

Kayleigh studied him, noting the black hair, blue eyes, and pale white skin. He looked like he could be Bridget's brother, but he seemed like a jumpy cat scared of his own shadow.

"Bridget?" Kayleigh repeated.

He sighed, and the blue of his eyes deepened with the sheen of tears. He shook his head slightly, opened and closed his mouth, and seemed to be warring with himself. He stared at Kayleigh and finally spoke.

"My name is Padraig Byrne O'Meara." His voice sounded deeper than Bridget's, but had her familiar lilt. "But I prefer Bridget."

"You're Bridget? Bridget Byrne?" Kayleigh blinked, trying to shake off the dream she must be having.

"You can call me Byrne if it's easier for you when I'm in this form...my original form." He grimaced when he spoke the word original, and he covered his face with his hands. "I was born male."

Kayleigh had accepted that Bridget was a shape-shifter, but the fact she was actually a boy was harder to comprehend. "So you disguised yourself as a girl to get closer to me?"

"It wasn't a disguise. I am a girl!" He lifted his head and defiantly raised his chin. "I was born in the wrong body, and I've hated myself since I was five. You wouldn't understand."

"So explain it to me, Byrne." Kayleigh kept her voice calm and even, not wanting to further antagonize her frenemy who now outweighed and outmuscled her.

He rocked forward and in one fluid motion rose to stand six feet tall. The dress that had previously reached Bridget's knees now skimmed the top of the boy's thighs. He placed one foot slightly in front of the other and rested one hand on his hip. Kayleigh saw a male teenager standing exactly as Bridget had only moments before.

"I was only five when I asked to be called Bridget. My *Daidi*...my father...looked at me like I'd just grown another head." Byrne dropped his arms, and his head fell forward. His voice grew soft. "*Daidi* was a tall burly man, the kind who'd put in hard days work in the mine. Then every night he'd leave my mother at home to get drunk in the pub and hit on the barmaids. He couldn't understand why one of his sons would want to be a girl."

He paced with smooth strides and wrung his hands together. His body swayed slightly back and forth with each graceful step, reminding her of Bridget. Gone, however, was the arrogance and confidence from the hallway. Like a thermal imager reads a heat signature, Kayleigh picked up waves of nervous energy radiating off his body.

"I suffered for years looking down at my male... body, knowing it wasn't right. I would sneak off and dress in my sisters' clothing, but my father would somehow find me and rip the dresses right off my body. He called me names like Nancy boy. Told me I was a disgrace."

Byrne crossed his arms over his chest in a self-protective gesture. "He sent me into the fields to work with my brothers when I was only ten years old. He would push me and say, 'That's where ye belong.'"

He looked at Kayleigh, and his cobalt eyes glistened in the lights of the gymnasium. "I couldn't be myself at home, so when I turned thirteen I ran away. I did odd jobs wherever I could to earn money, and I slept in barns."

Kayleigh imagined a boy with Bridget's blue eyes alone and scared, begging for food and work.

"Then, when I didn't think things could get worse, I hit puberty, and my body started changing into that of a man. I hated myself. Soon, I thought it might just be better to end my life."

He stopped pacing and ran a hand through his short hair. He looked down at the dress, one shoulder tattered, that stretched across his frame. "I haven't seen this form in such a long time."

He ran a palm lightly over a bicep and tugged at the edge of one sleeve. "I hate this body." He dropped his head to his chest and stroked the hair on his head.

"After a while, I'd had enough. I was sitting by the road one day, plotting how to kill myself, when a woman walked by. On the surface, she looked like any ordinary female, although I thought she was the most elegant woman I'd ever seen. She looked straight at me for several moments, just staring, and then said, 'Hello, Bridget.' It shocked me right out o' me shoes. I thought I must have gone blooming bonkers."

He approached Kayleigh and bent down in front of her. Byrne's face, streaked with tears, became intense, and his brow dug a deep line in between his eyebrows.

Kayleigh pressed herself against the wall, and her breath came in short pants. Pain radiated from her arm, and nausea rolled in her stomach, threatening to bring up her dinner.

"She was a morph but also a diviner." Byrne dropped on both knees and took Kayleigh's right hand. His skin scratched the back of her hand, rough and calloused. "A diviner can see a person's purest form. Fionnuala could see my true self, a female, and she saw that I had powers I hadn't discovered yet. She took me in. When I started changing into a morph, she taught me control."

Empathy welled in Kayleigh, and she imagined how hard that must have been.

"She was the first person who ever actually accepted me." Byrne's face softened, and Kayleigh suddenly saw her best friend again.

Kayleigh let him gently help her up, and he looked at her elbow. Several expressions flickered over his face, too quickly to read. "I'm sorry you're hurt." His concern jolted Kayleigh back to reality.

"Physically or emotionally?" Kayleigh asked and yanked her hand out of his. She took several steps back and held out one palm. "You harassed me, and I can't so quickly forget that, or forgive you simply because you were tormented by your father."

"I know," he said and lowered his head to look at the floor. "I had no right to...pay it forward. I was angry."

"You're a hypocrite," Kayleigh said, her anger building. "You were encouraging me to stand up for myself against Emma, but you never stood up to your father."

Byrne winced as if Kayleigh had punched him in the stomach, and she regretted her harsh words. There was a big difference between a fifteen-year-old mean girl and a fully-grown man. Fathers were supposed to protect and care for their children, not ridicule and bully them.

"I'm sorry. I shouldn't have said that." Kayleigh walked to the bleachers and sat. Her body ached from fighting, morphing, and falling. She attempted a smile. "So...you've been a guy this whole time?"

"Technically," Byrne answered. He perched on the bench several feet from Kayleigh. "But I've always felt like a girl."

"Does that mean you're gay?"

"No, sexuality and gender are two different things." He ran the backs of his hands across his eyes to wipe away the remaining tears. "If I ask for your gender on a form, for example, you mark..."

"Female." Kayleigh finished his sentence.

"Well, I do, too," Byrne said. "No matter what my body looks like."

"Okay." Kayleigh snuck a glance at her watch. Five minutes left before Daiyu and Ben would come looking for her. She wondered where the janitor had gone.

"So then, sexual orientation is separate from that," Byrne continued. "For example, you're a girl who likes boys. Heterosexual."

"Nate," Kayleigh said. She smiled to herself, and a flush of happiness warmed her.

"Again, so am I. A girl who likes boys." He paused and took a breath. "Some people are not going to understand, and they'll say that I'm gay. They'll see me as a boy attracted to other boys, like Ma—" He cut himself off and cleared his throat. "I mean, there are those guys who are comfortable being male and like other boys."

Kayleigh nodded but wondered whom he meant.

"I'm a trans girl." He suddenly smiled at her and his body relaxed. "I'm transgender."

Kayleigh followed his explanation. She smiled back. "And how old are you, exactly?"

"I'm only seventeen, actually," Byrne said. "I was recruited about a year after I first morphed, and they sent me here. I took it as an opportunity to be my true self." He pushed himself off the bleachers and stretched. With a shudder and a glint of light, his form shrunk and shifted back into Bridget's. Her dress now hung slightly off her shoulders, having been stretched and torn on one side.

"See, this is really me. I'm Bridget Byrne, female." She walked to where her pumps had fallen off. Her hair tumbled over her face when she bent to put them on. A radiant smile lit up her face when she righted herself on two high heels. "These are the shoes I was meant to wear."

Kayleigh looked at Bridget and saw both her best friend and someone who had lied to her and bullied her.

"I think I understand. I can accept that you're transgender—your gender doesn't match with your body. I can accept that your name is Bridget." Kayleigh paused and indignation returned. "What I can't comprehend is that you lied to me. And I'm not talking about your gender. I'm talking about being a morph. If you understood how hard it was, why wouldn't you help me? I don't buy the 'bully it forward' bull."

Bridget frowned, wrinkles deepening between her eyebrows. "I don't know." She paced back and forth several times, her heels clicking rapidly on the smooth gym floor. "Jealousy, I suppose. I watched your body change into a woman, and I envied you."

She ran her fingers over her hips and pivoted to face Kayleigh.

"I will always have to use powers to keep this form, and yet you come by your curves naturally. I bottled that anger for years until you started morphing."

"So you justified your actions by pretending to toughen me up?" Kayleigh asked.

"I'm sorry." Bridget drifted towards the exit.

Kayleigh's eyes followed her and caught sight of the drawing on the floor. Her face stared up at her from the parchment—an assignment from the kidnappers.

"Wait, please. You have to tell me what you know about my mother."

Bridget paused by the exit. "I don't know much, really. I know that she is alive and held captive by people you do not want to mess with. I heard stories about them making morphs disappear who were too outspoken in the organization, like your mom. There is some sort of hierarchy of leaders with their headquarters in Dublin, I think, but there are rumors of a castle-like stronghold somewhere in the country. I really only had contact with Fionnuala, and she relayed messages from her superiors. I have delayed giving them a status report, but I have to tell them something."

"Like what?" Kayleigh asked.

"Like you have started The Change, the Morphosis, but you don't know anything about your mother, and nothing about me."

"Will they come for me?" Goose bumps broke out on her arms, and she wrapped them around her torso.

"Not yet. Not as long as you're not a threat." There was a thud in the distance and shouting. Animal control or the police must have arrived.

Bridget looked up, her eyes widened, and she ran towards the exit. "I have to leave, now, and don't tell anyone you know your mother is still alive." She lifted one finger to her lips, and her blue eyes pleaded with Kayleigh. "Stay quiet, please, Kayleigh. Don't go looking for answers because the less you know, the safer you are. I never did want any harm to come to you."

She pushed the door handle and stepped outside as her black hair morphed into black feathers, and her arms changed into wings.

"Don't leave," Kayleigh cried. She pushed off the bench and held her injured arm to her side. "I still have too many questions." She ran after Bridget and tried to grab her arm as Bridget's form stretched, shimmered, and morphed into a large black swan.

Kayleigh tripped as the swan lifted off the surface and into the air. She landed on the concrete outside the door with a thud and rolled to the side. A fresh wave of pain pulsed in her side. She looked up, and the silhouette of a large swan against the moon gracefully sailed away on the summer night's breeze.

She slowly stood and glanced down at her hand. She was holding a black feather. It gleamed black with glints of blue in the moonlight, and then shimmered into several strands of black hair and blew away on the wind. *Magic.*

"Kayleigh, are you okay?" Daiyu and Ben shouted for her in the distance.

"Everything changes," she said softly to herself, quoting her mother's letter. "Everything."

CHAPTER FOURTEEN

FAMILY

Several weeks after her morph battle with Bridget, Kayleigh sat outside on the deck off the sun porch, enjoying the June sunshine from a lounge chair. Summer had arrived, and gentle breezes of eighty degrees warmed her skin and tickled the ruffle on her peasant blouse. *Delicious.*

A tall glass of iced tea stood on a small wooden table next to her recliner. Brightly colored flowers—sunny daffodils, rosy tulips, and fuchsia pansies—contrasted with the deep green lawn of the backyard, lush and teeming with life. Only one week in the school year remained.

Bridget had missed several weeks of school. She didn't come back after Kayleigh had confronted her, and the official story was that her family needed her to return to Ireland, but she could make up the work to pass the ninth grade. Kayleigh knew the truth. Bridget had left to report to a member of the secret society of morphs, the one nobody seemed to know anything about. She wondered if Bridget had kept her promise to only mention the bare minimum about Kayleigh.

So many questions remained unanswered about the parent organization that had sent Bridget here to spy. Perhaps they thought they had sent over a teenaged boy who could win Kayleigh over with charm and good looks, but Padraig O'Meara had done much better as herself, a girl named Bridget Byrne.

Kayleigh stretched her legs out on the lounge chair and surveyed her body. She couldn't imagine waking up every day and hating what she saw. She didn't like everything about being a woman, especially once a month, but at least she knew she was supposed to be female. Her outsides matched her insides. Although she supposed it wasn't even as simple as that. People rarely ever fit neatly into categories, no matter how hard society tried.

She took a sip of tea. Sweet sugar and lemon slid down her throat, cooling and soothing. Her unopened biology book lay on a larger table nearby with her notebook and pens. She was supposed to be studying for her biology final but questions about her own anatomy clambered for attention.

Several months ago she would have said that all humans on earth belonged to the species *Homo sapiens,* but morphs clearly didn't fit into this box. Kayleigh needed to know more about how morphs had been created. The information in her mother's chest only explained the legend of the Children of Lir and how their stepmother turned them into swans with dark magic. She wanted more details on the dark magic itself.

Kayleigh also wanted to know who belonged to the society. If they were all morphs, did they also have day jobs? Maybe they used their powers for illegal purposes, such as impersonating public figures or robbing bank accounts. Certainly an organization that kidnapped women wasn't all good. If Bridget and Anne didn't have the answers, then she would have to find who did.

Kayleigh wondered where Bridget fell on the spectrum of good and bad. The secret society had given her a vague assignment to go watch a young girl, and for over two years, it was an opportunity to actually be a girl.

Her first memory of Bridget flooded into her head, blurring her vision. She had stood on the blacktop in front of Emma, the hot sun beating down on her hair, while Emma called her a spic-mix. When Kayleigh told her father, he turned red and had said between clenched teeth that she probably meant mixed race, including Hispanic.

Kayleigh hadn't even considered she was different from her classmates. At least, not until Emma introduced doubt and trampled on her self-esteem.

That day during recess, Bridget had stepped in and defended Kayleigh. The first time of many. Her exact words were "*Oi*, blondie, stuff it and leave 'er alone." When Emma persisted, asking Bridget if she even spoke English, Bridget shoved her and said, "Understand that?"

Kayleigh smiled, remembering how Emma had landed on her bottom in the gravel, her mouth gaping open at Bridget.

A rustle in the trees brought her out of her reverie, and she saw a familiar blue-black shine from an upper branch.

"Bridget, I know it's you," Kayleigh called to the raven.

The huge bird flew behind a tree, and a second later Bridget appeared. She hesitated by the trunk, her sapphire eyes studying Kayleigh. She wore a turquoise tank top and faded jeans, her ivory skin flushed with pink. Her dark hair spilled around her shoulders and partially covered her face.

"You're back," Kayleigh said.

Bridget crossed to the edge of the steps leading to the deck and paused. A deep groove formed between her perfectly manicured eyebrows.

"You might as well come on up, unless you're planning to turn into a grizzly bear to take on my tiger." Kayleigh took another sip of tea and exhaled slowly, fighting a surge of defensive anger.

Kayleigh hadn't completely forgiven Bridget for sending her anonymous threats, but she had somehow accepted Bridget's twisted logic without judgment. Mindfulness was to thank for that.

She empathized with and understood jealousy. Kayleigh had always been jealous of Bridget's long hair, superior height, and curvaceous figure. Turns out, Bridget was envious of Kayleigh's body and natural womanhood. *The grass is always greener.*

Bridget stepped up the deck stairs, her sandals clip-clopping on the wood. She settled in a lounge chair near Kayleigh, tucking her legs underneath her. She gazed out on the lawn in silence, and a lost look flitted over her face.

"I'm sorry." When she finally spoke, her voice shook and tears teetered on the edges of her dark lashes.

"I know." Kayleigh paused, not sure what to say. She wanted to forget the entire first year of high school had happened and go back to when she and Bridget were just two girls. Best friends. "I've missed you."

Bridget let out a long sigh. "I've missed you, too. You're still my best friend."

"But you betrayed me." Kayleigh's voice seemed flat as she repressed anger and pain.

"I did." Bridget sniffed and pulled a tissue out of her pocket. "When I was first given your picture, and Fionnuala said I was going to America, I saw it as a chance to be a whole new me. The real me."

Kayleigh shifted in her chair, still uncomfortable with the idea she had been an assignment. She set her tea back on the table and watched the ice cubes bob and rise to the surface.

Bridget dabbed at her eyes with the tissue and continued. "That first week I wasn't sure how to approach you, and then ironically Emma provided the way. She was so mean...she reminded me of my father."

"So why get nasty yourself?" Kayleigh said.

Bridget picked at invisible lint on the edge of her jeans. "It felt good to push Emma that first time. I could finally fight back."

"So pick on those who deserve it, like Emma." A strong breeze pulled several strands of auburn hair out of her ponytail and whipped them across her face.

"I guess jealousy...like I said." Bridget tucked her long hair behind her ears and shrugged. A pink flush darkened her cheeks.

"Clearly you've mastered your powers enough to get the body you want," Kayleigh said. "In fact, I should have you teach me. There are some days I'd also like to be a supermodel."

Bridget chuckled. "I don't think it's just jealousy that you're naturally female," Bridget said. "It's more than that. You have everything—a father who cares for you, friends, love."

Kayleigh processed Bridget's words for a moment. Her mother's disappearance had left such a gaping hole that it overshadowed the fact she still had a parent who loved and cared for her, which was more than Bridget had.

"My father cares for you as well," Kayleigh said. "He knows you're my best friend and were...are...important to me."

Bridget had become her best friend almost three years ago, even though Kayleigh had known Ben and Daiyu since elementary school. The three of them had picked up the quiet and kind Natalie along the way. Martin was a more recent addition to their group, ever since he and Kayleigh had been paired up for a science project last year. Kayleigh always wondered why he wasn't better friends with the football players. When Bridget had arrived, their motley crew easily expanded to accept her.

"You have friends, too." Kayleigh smiled. "Ben has asked me every day when you plan on returning. He's trying to practice "good morning" in Irish Gaelic, but I suspect he's butchering it."

Bridget laughed, and for a moment Kayleigh forgot about the anonymous messages and epic morph battle. She stared out at the lush lawn, and the sun warmed her face. A breeze played with the loose strands of hair around her face, and condensation formed on the outside of her glass. For a moment, she pretended none of ninth grade had happened and they were all still friends.

"What did you tell them?" Bridget's smile faded, and she tugged at the bottom of her shirt.

"What did I tell our friends about you?" Kayleigh sighed. "I had to tell them you sent all of the nasty texts and Nonys, but I told them you were trying to toughen me up for Emma. And that it worked."

Bridget let out a long exhale and sat back against the recliner, unfolding her long legs. Kayleigh studied Bridget's face. The dark hair, arched cheek bones, thick lashes, and deep blue of her eyes were so similar to her male form, it seemed unfair that mother nature had not made her a girl.

"I left out the part about morphing," Kayleigh said. "I told them we ran into the crazed dog and cat fight, and it trapped us in the gym until the animal control people came."

Bridget winced. "How did they react?"

"Daiyu just looked confused, Natalie was quiet, and Martin talked about how breaking laws to right wrongs was still breaking laws. Ben didn't seem too concerned and said something about cool psychological warfare with a stupid grin on his face. You know Ben."

Bridget rolled her head to the side and surveyed Kayleigh. "So you really didn't tell them anything about morphing?"

"No, not yet." Kayleigh hated keeping secrets from her friends, but defying the laws of physics was not something to reveal in casual conversation.

"You can't. It would put everyone in danger." Bridget leaned forward

"From whom?" Kayleigh turned to face Bridget directly and stared into her eyes. "The secret organization that sent you to spy on me? The same one that may have kidnapped my mother?"

Bridget looked down, and scarlet flushed her high cheekbones.

"Who are they?" Kayleigh pressed.

"I only met a small circle of morphs outside Dublin. Only ones that Fionnuala introduced me to."

"And you told them what, exactly?"

"Just that I saw you shimmer with a morph, but that you didn't really get very far." She fiddled with the frayed edge of a hole over her knee.

"So what did they say?" Kayleigh frowned, impatient with Bridget's vague answers. The desire to know more created rapid fire questions that buzzed in her head like a swarm of bees.

"Just that they'll report back to their superiors," Bridget said.

"Who are the leaders?" Kayleigh asked.

"I honestly don't know. They didn't appreciate the questions, and I think the organization keeps themselves compartmentalized so no one has too much information."

"Like terrorist cells. Great." Kayleigh couldn't keep the sarcasm from coating her words.

"But I didn't mention your mother's things..." Bridget averted her eyes, and Kayleigh read guilt moving over her face. "Or Anne."

"You know about Anne?" Kayleigh pressed her lips together tightly, small lines forming between her chin and bottom lip. "So that was you. The raven overlooking the garden."

Bridget nodded, and she glanced up at Kayleigh under a fringe of dark lashes. "I saw your blue jay imitation. Not bad at all."

"Thanks."

Bridget shifted in her chair. "Right up until you landed in the fountain."

Kayleigh covered her face and groaned. "Oh, you saw that, too?"

"A bird is a harder form to master than land mammals. There's the whole learning to fly, and you did surprisingly well for your first time."

"That's what Anne said." Kayleigh adjusted the neckline of her shirt, retying the tassels of the peasant top.

"I'd like to meet her."

"Good, because I didn't tell our friends about morphs, but I did tell Anne and my father everything that happened. Anne and Dad were both shocked you were a morph spy."

Bridget slunk down in the seat and pulled her knees up to her chest. "I'm sorry," she mumbled into her jeans.

"They seemed less surprised when I told them you were born male," Kayleigh said. "I guess they understood with the power of morphing comes the desire to reinvent oneself."

Bridget picked up her head and studied Kayleigh. "You can morph into anyone you want. Who do you want to be?"

Kayleigh swung her legs over the edge of her chair and faced Bridget. "Me. I just want to be me."

"Me too," Bridget said, her eyes watering.

"In my case it's easier to figure out who I am without adding morphing to the mix," Kayleigh said. "But I understand that in your case, you found the real you through morphing."

Bridget nodded and uncurled her legs.

In one swift motion, Kayleigh pushed herself off the lounge chair and held out a hand. "So, let's put everything behind us and start again."

Bridget put her hand in Kayleigh's and stood. "In that case I have one more thing to tell you."

Kayleigh paused. "Should I sit back down?"

"It's not that big." Bridget walked to the railing and looked out at the lawn. "I told Fionnuala and the morphs that I revealed myself to you."

"As a morph or as male?" Kayleigh asked.

"Both. They were a little upset I didn't keep an element of surprise." Bridget's shoulders slumped, and she fiddled with one spaghetti strap.

"Believe me. I was surprised." Kayleigh joined her at the railing, the wood smooth beneath her fingers.

"I told them it was so I could gain your trust and get more information about your skills."

"In order to do what, exactly?"

"Nothing yet. I'm just supposed to stay close and watch." Bridget shifted her weight on her sandals and sighed. "And report back about your progress."

"As a morph?" Kayleigh wondered if they thought she was as much of a threat as her mother had apparently been.

"Yeah, how skillful you are." Bridget paused and looked at Kayleigh out of the corner of her eye. "If you've told anyone."

"Only my father." Kayleigh blew a lock of hair out of her face and turned towards Bridget. She leaned one hip against the railing and hooked an arm over the edge.

Bridget nodded and traced the grain of the wood with her fingernail. "They can't know he knows, Kayleigh, okay? They probably assumed that your mom didn't tell him, which is why they didn't take him, too."

Kayleigh shuddered and wrapped her arms around her chest. "I need to find my mom. You have to help me."

"I know. I will." Bridget slung one arm around Kayleigh, who let her head fall to one side on Bridget's shoulder. "I'm a double agent now."

Kayleigh laughed, and the last of the anger faded away, leaving only relief that Bridget was still her best friend.

Later that week, Kayleigh's father prepared a dinner for the morphs, and he, Anne, and Kayleigh sat talking, waiting for Bridget to arrive. He made jokes about having three morphs together, but Kayleigh could tell he was worried.

He'd recently adjusted to the idea Mrs. O'Neill was actually his missing wife's cousin Anne, and they'd gotten reacquainted over tea. Kayleigh had savored hearing their stories of her mother. Her father's face had showed less pain and more hope when Anne suggested her mother was still alive. Now, he had to accept his daughter's best friend as a transgender morph.

Anne had not been happy to learn that Bridget had been spying on them, or that the society had sent her after Kayleigh. The evening of the dinner, the three of them sat at the wooden table in the kitchen, late afternoon sunlight streaming in from the windows, and Anne expressed concern that bringing the spy into the house posed risks to all of them.

"I understand your concerns, Anne," Kayleigh said. She ran a hand through her hair and adjusted the clasp of the key necklace at the back of her neck. "But Bridget had several years in and out of this house to cause me physical harm, and she only ever used technology. Besides, she and I fought, epic style. Then we talked it over and made up. It's now water under the bridge."

"Her animosity of you may be, but who knows how the secret society wants to use her to get information?" Anne asked.

"I know there is still a huge unknown." Kayleigh rose at the heavy thud of knocking on the mudroom door. "But the undisclosed part isn't Bridget."

Kayleigh paused at the kitchen door and glanced back at Anne and her father, who whispered to each other, heads bent. Dusk spilled in and bathed the adults in a coral glow.

She took a deep breath and entered the mudroom. They would need to hear it firsthand from Bridget to believe she'd changed. She opened the door and motioned for Bridget to enter.

"Hey." Bridget stepped inside and smoothed her pleated sundress with trembling hands.

"Hi. Are you ready?"

Bridget nodded, her unease evident in the lines marring her forehead.

"It'll be okay." Kayleigh gave her a quick hug and a smile she hoped was reassuring. She entered the kitchen, and the atmosphere seemed to have cooled several degrees. Both adults were standing next to the table, their faces solemn.

"Dad, you know Bridget already."

"Mostly," he said in a hushed tone.

Kayleigh laughed, a strained cackling that grated even on her ears. She took a breath and willed the awkward feeling to recede, shrugging one shoulder. "How well does anybody really know each other?"

Anne cleared her throat and pointedly looked at Kayleigh.

"Anne, meet Bridget," Kayleigh said, waving her hand back and forth. "Bridget, this is Anne."

Anne moved her eyes up and down Bridget's form, seemingly to conduct a silent appraisal of Kayleigh's best friend. Bridget's cheeks now shone as red as apples on her ivory skin, and she fidgeted with her dress under Anne's scrutiny.

"Good evening," Bridget said. Her voice wavered slightly.

"*Tráthnóna maith.*" Anne returned the greeting in Irish Gaelic.

"Well, we'll let the two of you get acquainted," Kayleigh said. "Dad and I have dinner to finish."

"Thank you, Kayleigh. Bridget and I will talk out on the deck." She took several steps away from the window and out of sight of anyone peering in from the outside. As she motioned for Bridget to join her, she morphed into her public persona, Mrs. O'Neill, and conversed with Bridget in Irish Gaelic. They disappeared into the living room and reappeared moments later out on the deck.

The sun had slipped behind the horizon; shades of ruby red and purple streaked the sky. Kayleigh wondered if her mother saw the same colors, and a ripple of longing originated in her heart.

Kayleigh joined her father by the cutting board where he prepared dinner. He added diced onions, pepper, and garlic to the chili simmering on the stove. Kayleigh picked up a clove of garlic. "Geez, Dad, we're morphs, not vampires."

"Very funny." He added in cheese and ground beef, stirring the chili mixture with a wooden spoon.

He gestured outside to Mrs. O'Neill and Bridget. "What do you suppose they're saying?"

"I suppose they're comparing notes," Kayleigh said. "Anne is probably asking questions about the people who sent Bridget, and Bridget is probably asking Anne if she knows Fionnuala. We're all wondering about the mysterious man who gave Anne the key to Mom's chest."

"Do you suppose that's what they were looking for?" her father asked. He added chili powder, cumin, and cayenne pepper to the pot.

"What do you mean?" Kayleigh asked. She leaned over and inhaled the spices, her mouth watering.

"Well, I always wondered if they meant to kidnap your mother," he said. "Or even if roughing me up was part of the plan. Maybe we arrived home at the wrong time. Why did they trash the house if it was a simple kidnapping?"

"Of course," Kayleigh said, a flashbulb going off in her head. "They opened cabinets, slashed the sofa cushions, and pulled books off the shelves. They must have been looking for the chest that Mom had given Anne for safekeeping. The one she left for me on Christmas."

Kayleigh ran to her room, eager to get the chest and have another look at its contents. She took the stairs two at a time and threw open the door to her room. She slid on the rug and landed on the floor, peering under the bed. Her pulse quickened when she caught sight of the small wooden trunk with the Celtic carvings. She grabbed it and raced back downstairs, breathing heavily from the sprint.

Once inside the kitchen again, she took the key from around her neck and slid it into the keyhole. The chest opened with a small click. Her father adjusted his glasses and waited until she spread the contents on the table. She watched as he read through the letters from her mother, his eyes watering. He traced a finger on the drawings and studied the genealogy.

Kayleigh glanced outside to the two women conversing on the deck. The tone of their voices carried clearly into the kitchen through the open window, but Kayleigh understood zero Irish Gaelic.

Her father picked up the reading glasses and studied them for a moment. Kayleigh noticed the spectacles looked cruder than she remembered — nothing but uneven metal bent around two rough lenses. He shrugged and took off his own glasses, slipping her mother's on his face.

"How do I look?" He smiled at Kayleigh and gazed around the kitchen.

Suddenly he yelled and stumbled backwards into the kitchen island. Kayleigh followed the line of his vision outside, and her eyes locked onto Mrs. O'Neill and Bridget. They heard his startled yelp and came inside through the sunroom.

When they entered the kitchen, her father took off the glasses and sat down at the table, breathing heavily.

"Cedro, what is it?" Mrs. O'Neill knelt down in front of him and took one of his hands in hers.

"Dad, are you okay?" Kayleigh slid onto the bench next to him.

He ran a hand through his hair and a little chuckle escaped his lips. He passed Kayleigh the reading glasses. "I'm fine. Just surprised. Have a look."

Kayleigh hesitated, glancing at Mrs. O'Neill and Bridget. She slid on the glasses and looked at her father. He placed a hand on her chin and turned her head to look at their guests.

When Kayleigh looked through the glasses, a young Anne, not Mrs. O'Neill, knelt next to her father, and Byrne the boy stood nearby, a sheen surrounding each of them. The figures weren't entirely clear, but a shadow of their original forms showed through the morph. Kayleigh jumped and blinked.

"Now we can guess what they were looking for," Kayleigh said.

Anne took the glasses off Kayleigh's face, and she once again appeared clearly as Mrs. O'Neill. She slipped them on and looked at Bridget. "I would say that's correct."

Mrs. O'Neill handed them to Bridget, who put them on and looked back at her, and her eyebrows lifted over the rim of the glasses in surprise. She then looked down at herself and groaned. She put the glasses back on the table and plopped down across from Kayleigh.

"Morphs wouldn't be able to hide from anyone who wore these," Bridget said.

Mrs. O'Neill drew the curtains. She morphed into Anne, tightened the sash on her dress, and sat next to Bridget.

"I imagine this is why Órla was a target," Anne said.

"What do we do?" Kayleigh asked.

"Nothing for now," Anne said. "We still need to keep a low profile."

"They'll be coming—" Bridget said.

"Bridget." Anne cut her off.

"Kayleigh needs to know," Bridget insisted. "It's partially my fault. I was sent here to watch her."

"And you'll continue to do exactly that," Anne said. "Give them reports that Kayleigh hasn't fully changed yet, and that will give us time to plan."

"I say bring it." Kayleigh stood up and placed her hands on her hips. "I'm ready for whatever. Bridget did an excellent job of vaccinating me against threats."

Her father gave Bridget a disapproving look. She ducked her head.

"Dad, stop. Bridget and I got past that, and although the effort was misguided, I was able to stand up to Emma. I'm not afraid of what might be coming."

Anne raised one eyebrow at her. A cold wave of apprehension licked along Kayleigh's spine. She paused and listened to her body, using mindfulness to recognize the fear that danced along her skin. She took a deep breath and let it slowly recede. "Well, I am afraid, but I won't let it run my life."

"I agree," Anne said. "This has been a difficult enough year without worrying about what might be."

"So then, let's eat," Kayleigh said. She ladled bowls of steaming hot chili and allowed the fear to slowly fade. She looked at her family, which now included Anne and Bridget, and a warm swirl of contentment replaced her worry.

CHAPTER FIFTEEN

FLY

M r. Rhodes took attendance, even though it was the last day of school. "Congratulations, students, on surviving your first year of high school."

Kayleigh smiled at the cheers that broke out in the classroom. Ben jumped up and gave Nate a high five, letting out a whoop. Emma snorted and looked down her nose at him, but he scrunched up his face and crossed his eyes at her in response.

A giggle escaped Kayleigh, drawing Emma's stare. For a moment they locked eyes in a game of chicken. Kayleigh refused to look away, and Emma's face reddened slowly like a sunburn. Emma blinked and looked away. Pride rushed over Kayleigh like the water through open floodgates on a dam. She really could defend herself.

The morning went quickly as several classes consisted only of watching a movie while cleaning out the classrooms. The rising sophomore class voted to watch the computer hacker flick that had been in the theaters in February, which had just been released on DVD. It was the same movie she had seen with Nate on her first date. She had been so nervous that night, unprepared to handle all the feelings that overwhelmed her. How things had changed.

The bell rang and signaled lunch, which was the last period of the day in her schedule because of early dismissal. She stepped into the hallway, which wasn't any less crowded on the last day.

Several large trashcans had been placed at equal intervals in the hallways for students to empty out their lockers. Kayleigh trod gingerly along the minefield and gripped her bag, dodging students who chucked papers, old binders, and projects into the trash.

She paused at the nurse's office on her way to the lunchroom, and the sight of Mrs. Rouhani inside sent a pang of guilt shooting through her. She remembered the scene in the kitchen and how she'd been rude to a woman who'd been nothing but kind.

The door opened with a gust of air scented with antiseptic and pistachios. Mrs. Rouhani turned, her long braid swinging across her back. Her eyebrows, which arched delicately over her dark eyes, curved further when she saw Kayleigh.

"Kayleigh, *Joon*, are you ill?" Mrs. Rouhani asked. She hurried to her visitor and brushed the hair away from her eyes. Warmth crept over Kayleigh's face. "You look flushed."

"I'm fine. I just stopped by to say I'm sorry." Kayleigh realized she had missed the soothing presence of the nurse. "For being rude to you."

"You don't have to apologize." Mrs. Rouhani shook her head and motioned for her to sit down. "You were protecting your father."

Kayleigh sat next to the nurse and chose her words carefully. "I know Dad's lonely, but my mother is still alive." She grabbed one of Mrs. Rouhani's hands. "I know she is."

Mrs. Rouhani's dark eyes roamed over Kayleigh's face, and she smiled. "Of course she is, my dear." She patted Kayleigh's hand, and her smile faded.

"Well, I can't stay," Kayleigh stood and shifted the bag on her shoulder. "I just wanted to say have a good summer."

"And you, as well."

"I'll see you in the fall." Kayleigh opened the door and entered the bedlam of the hallway. Several students played catch with the skeletal head off an anatomy display. She ducked as the skull soared over her head, and grinning teeth gleamed in the fluorescent lights.

Kayleigh reached the lunchroom, and the familiar roar of gossiping students competed with the rumble of kitchen equipment and the clatter of dishes.

She found her friends sitting together at a long table, and she slid in between Bridget and Nate, who gave her a kiss on the temple.

"Hey, guys," Kayleigh said. She pulled out a small Tupperware bowl and a spoon from her lunchbox. Her father's chili tasted even more delicious as cold leftovers. "So what's everyone doing this summer?"

"We're going to spend a month in China," Daiyu said. "We'll visit both my parents' families." She sighed and opened her thermos.

"That sounds exciting," Kayleigh said. "So why do you look like you just announced you have summer school?"

"Because they signed me up for a Chinese dance summer camp." Daiyu's shoulders slumped, and she stared at her lunch. "I can't possibly compete with girls who have been trained in China."

"Come on, D," Ben said. "You know you're an amazing dancer."

Daiyu's eyes lit up, and she smiled at Ben. "You really think so?"

"Uh, of course." Ben stammered and pulled at his collar. He quickly changed topics. "What about you, Nate?"

"Boy Scout Camp for me."

"So you'll be hanging out with a bunch of sweaty boys in the woods all summer?" Bridget asked. She grinned at Nate and winked at Martin.

"Ha ha, Bridget." Nate smirked at her. "I'll learn survival skills, such as starting fires, building shelter, and finding food."

"Perfect for when the zombie apocalypse hits," Natalie said. She peered at Nate over the top of her computer and giggled.

He chuckled and puffed up his chest. "I'll also go to lacrosse camp the second half of the summer."

"Brains and brawn," Kayleigh leaned over and planted a kiss on his cheek. "Adorable...I just wish it wasn't all summer."

"I promise to write lots of letters."

Kayleigh sighed. "What about you, Martin?"

"I'm doing a summer football training camp over at the college," he said.

"I'll be there, too," Natalie said. "Not for the football, but for summer classes. I'm taking one on computers and participating in the Hackathon."

"More hacking?" Bridget raised an eyebrow.

"It's more like an app building competition," Natalie said. "We're allowed to use any public API—application programming interface—and hardware they provide to build our own apps."

"What are you going to build?" Ben asked.

"I want to build a mobile device that counteracts the anonymous feature on Nony. I think if people want to say something, they shouldn't hide behind social media, even if the point of Nony is to be anonymous."

Kayleigh froze and glanced between Bridget and her friends. She'd explained to them what had happened with Bridget, minus the morphing part, but no one had outwardly mentioned the anonymous torment meant to toughen Kayleigh up. An awkward silence covered the table, which contrasted with the cacophony of the lunchroom.

Bridget finally broke the silence. "Amen, Natalie." She threw an arm around Kayleigh and gave her a brief squeeze. "Not many kids are as tough as our girl, here. Hack 'em all."

Natalie let out a long exhale, and a Mona Lisa smile crept over her face. "Ben, you haven't mentioned what you're doing this summer."

"I'm going to visit some relatives in Manhattan for a couple of weeks," he said. "We'll probably hang out in Central Park and visit some museums." He took a bite of pizza. "And later I'll join Nate and the guys for some camping."

"Going from uptown dinners to campfires under the moonlight, Ben?" Bridget asked. She gave him a wink and a sardonic smile. "I had no idea you could fit in with both."

"Clearly." Ben narrowed his eyes at Bridget. "And what about you?"

"I'm not doing much this summer, other than hanging out with Kayleigh. Since I was just in Ireland, I won't make the trip again so soon."

"So you'll stay here, and we can do some training," Kayleigh said to Bridget.

"What kind of training, Kayleigh?" Martin asked. Bridget's eyes widened, and she shook her head slightly at Kayleigh.

"I'd like to train in tai chi," Kayleigh said. "Maybe some Buddhist meditation." She looked pointedly at her friend.

Bridget laughed. "Yes, that sounds like a relaxing way to spend a summer. Throw in some manicures and facials, and I'm in."

Kayleigh chuckled and dug into her chili. She hoped that her summer would be less exciting than the school year had been.

As soon as the bell had rung announcing the end of 9th grade, Kayleigh and Bridget followed the wooded path that connected the school to the nearby park. Kayleigh wanted to watch the swans and ducks on the lake before they met their friends for a celebratory dinner.

"Just so you know, I'm limiting us to three mani-pedis this summer," Kayleigh said as they walked through the woods, dense trees forming a canopy of green around them.

"You only say that because your feet are ticklish," Bridget said. She stepped around some moss and weeds that had grown up through a crack in the asphalt.

"True, but the idea is for us to train with Anne, not waste time in the spa."

Bridget mimicked a pampering at the spa. She brushed her hair back, lightly touched her face with her palms, and pretended to paint her nails.

Kayleigh grinned. "And I want to learn how to be a better morph."

Bridget stopped her pantomime. "Shh. I know that we agreed the secret society already knew about the two of us being morphs, but we don't need to tell all of Onondaga County."

"We're in an extremely secluded forest. No one is here. But what if I did let the secret slip, what would they do? Kidnap me?" Kayleigh asked. She looked around the forest and defiantly put her hands on her hips.

"Yes, exactly!" Bridget said. "So keep it down."

Kayleigh sobered. Conflict raged in her gut. If they kidnapped her, she might find her mother, but it would leave her father scared and alone. She acknowledged both the fear and desire to rebel competing in her chest.

"You know what the word morph is derived from?" Bridget asked.

"I'm guessing you're about to tell me," Kayleigh said, welcoming the change of subject. She grinned at Bridget and kicked a small pebble on the path. It skipped along the walkway and startled several doves, which cooed and fled into the bushes. "Oops."

"From the Latin *metamorphosis*," Bridget continued. "Meaning a major change in the appearance of something or in the form or structure of an animal or insect."

"I know. Like a frog or a butterfly."

"Well, it also means a change in character." Bridget glanced at Kayleigh, dipping her head. Her hair swung down like a curtain, hiding her eyes.

Kayleigh stopped walking and studied Bridget, who peered up through her lashes. Her lower lip trembled, and she wrung her hands together. Kayleigh read shame and remorse on her face as easily as if someone had stamped a scarlet A there.

"Enough." Kayleigh threw her arms around Bridget. "We already talked it over, and I forgave you. It was very hard for me, but I got through it."

"I can't get rid of this guilt," Bridget said. "I keep thinking I have to apologize over and over." She looked at Kayleigh, and the pain was evident—in her eyes, the wrinkle of her brow, the lines around her lips.

"Don't think about getting rid of it," Kayleigh said. "Accept it instead. You made a mistake, and you feel bad. If you didn't feel guilty, we'd have another problem."

A small giggle escaped Bridget's lips. Several small birds twittered in the forest, and the breeze rustled the trees. Sunlight peeped through the canopy, creating lines and circles of hazy sunlight on the forest floor.

Kayleigh put a hand on either side of Bridget's shoulders and gave her a small shake. "But the feeling is only temporary. Accept it for what it is, and it will gradually fade."

"Ah, so Anne's taught you mindfulness," Bridget said. She used a finger to dab at the corner of her eye.

"You know what else Anne's taught me?" Kayleigh stepped to one side of the path and took a deep breath. Her skin shimmered briefly and then whitened. Feathers sprouted out of her pores as her body plumped and white plumage replaced her hair and clothes. Her neck lengthened, and her nose and mouth morphed into a black bill. Kayleigh spread her arms and flapped two full wings, a beautiful white swan.

Bridget looked around at the forest, concern marring her perfect features. "Kayleigh..."

Kayleigh shook her body and morphed out of the swan. Her clothes slid into place, and she triumphantly hollered.

"One problem," Bridget said. She pointed to Kayleigh's T-shirt, which was now on backwards.

"Well, yeah. I'm still working out a couple of kinks," Kayleigh said. Her skin shimmered and stretched part way into a swan while she righted her shirt. "There."

"Didn't Anne tell us not to morph in public?"

"Public? We're in the middle of the woods. I'll refrain from morphing where there are actually other people present."

"They will be coming, you know." Bridget's face dropped. "The society."

"Let them come." Kayleigh morphed back into the white swan and spread her wings, letting the breeze flow through her feathers. She nudged Bridget with her beak, and her friend morphed into a black swan, her feathers glinting blue in the sunlight that streamed through the trees.

Kayleigh flapped her wings and lifted off the ground. Bridget followed. Kayleigh sailed through the trees towards the lake, preparing herself to land at the water's edge. The soul of the trumpeter coursed through her, bold yet graceful.

Let them come. I'm not a little girl anymore.

EPILOGUE
KIDNAPPED

THREE YEARS AGO

Pain radiated through Órla's arms, and she winced. She shifted her arms and tried to relieve the pressure of handcuffs pinching the soft skin of her wrists. She tried to dislodge the blindfold by shaking her head and scrapping the cloth's knot against the wall, but it stayed tight against her eyes.

They bumped along in some kind of vehicle—a truck, based on the rumble of the engine and the feel of metal slats underneath her bare calves.

They were moving her—where, she didn't know. She guessed they'd already traveled over ground to one of the ports in upstate New York, where she'd smelled seawater and heard gulls. They'd crossed the ocean by boat for at least a week, and luckily she hadn't gotten motion sickness. Once they'd docked somewhere over seas, they'd shoved her in the back of the current vehicle and had been traveling at least an hour. She strained against the handcuffs and gasped when a sharp edge of metal scratched her arm.

"Hold still and it won't hurt," a Scottish accent said from the front of the cab.

"Or better yet," a nasal Cockney accent said, "Struggle all you want and make it more painful. And more bloody."

Órla froze, and goose bumps sprung up on her forearms at the disdain oozing from his words. She sensed the challenge in the second man's words. He'd been one of the men to break into her Syracuse home.

The large burly man with a masochistic streak had orders from the demon to kidnap her, but she figured it was his idea of fun when he'd broken her husband's arm and bruised his face. She thought of Cedro, lying broken on his study floor and bit back a whimper. He'd tried to protect her, but his peaceful nature was no match for two henchmen shape-shifters.

Worse yet, Kayleigh had entered the side door seconds before the bigger guy pulled Órla out the back door. She'd heard her young daughter's voice, shaking and weak, calling from the tossed family room. Órla's chest tightened when she thought about the emotional damage that kind of trauma would cause a young girl — Kayleigh — *her* baby girl.

The truck lurched and bounced into a pothole, jolting Órla from her thoughts. She struggled against something that tied her feet, and a rough rope dug into the skin at her ankles. The instinctive urge to morph overwhelmed her senses.

The edges of change shimmered along her skin, and the image of a Eurasian jay popped into her mind, noisy and confident. She pictured the amber shades of the head and the blue and black checkerboard along the wings. Her arms started to morph into wings, but a sharp pain radiated from her wrists and stopped her mid-shift. Órla yelped and took a breath against the pain of a million pinpricks on each pore.

She sighed and softly cursed under her breath for having forgotten the spell, old and powerful, which emanated from the cold metal links. Órla knew the bracelet had been engraved with Celtic symbols to bind its power.

When she and Anne were teenagers, her grandmother had explained to them that the enchanted metal prevented the wearer from using morphing powers to change shapes. Órla couldn't effectively tap into her magic, and would be unable to sustain any morph, even with over thirty years of experience and skills as a shape-shifter.

She figured they couldn't erect a mystical barrier around a moving truck, so they'd stuck her back in anti-morph handcuffs.

The truck screeched to a halt, and doors slammed. The sharp footsteps of boots on concrete preceded the screech of a metal rod sliding to open the back doors. Air whooshed through the strands of hair sticking out from the cloth tied around her head and tickled her nose with the smell of damp earth and pine trees. Rough hands grabbed her upper arms and hauled her out of the back.

Someone grabbed the blindfold off her head, ripping out several strands of hair caught in the knot. She blinked against the harsh sunlight. Was it morning? As her eyes adjusted, she heard the call of mourning doves in the background and the chatter of sparrows and other small birds. The air, moist with dew, reminded Órla of her childhood in Laois Country, Ireland. Her eyes adjusted, and she noted the emerald green fields, colorful wildflowers dotting the rolling hills, and fluffy clouds sailing across a clear blue sky—Ireland. They'd brought her back to Ireland.

Her chest ached, not only for her homeland, but also because she'd been taken so far away from her husband and daughter in Syracuse, New York. She blinked back tears. It would not be helpful to lose her cool before she figured out what was happening.

To her left, a large stone castle rose out of the green hill. English ivy peppered the drab gray granite on either side of an arched oak door. A turret graced the top of each corner of the rectangular structure and a tall tower raised several stories above the roof. Guards stood watch along the walls, dressed in olive green khaki. They didn't appear to be armed, but Orlá knew they possessed an arsenal of magic to rival any handgun.

Two figures blocked her view and the sun on her face. The burly Englishman, a wide grin plastered on his face, stood next to a leanly muscled man with a carrot top of curls and matching scraggly beard—the Scot. He gently checked the handcuffs, and used a handkerchief to dab at a bloody cut on her wrist. The bigger man scoffed at his partner and walked off.

"Cedro's okay," the redhead whispered.

Órla's eyes widened, and shock rippled across her face. She whispered back. "And Kayleigh?"

"She bumped into me—literally—about half-a-minute after Roy pulled you out the back door." He sighed and tucked his handkerchief back in this pocket.

A gasp whooshed through Órla's lips.

"Kayleigh's fine," the Scot quickly said. "She—"

"*Oy*, what's the holdup, Georgie?" Roy called from the top of the path and gestured.

Georgie gave her an apologetic frown and guided her towards the entrance to the stronghold.

Órla longed to know more about her family. Would they be kidnapped as well? She got Georgie's attention and whispered. "Is my family in dang—"

"*Shh!* Not now." Georgie glanced nervously towards Roy.

As they neared the front gate, a sizzle of electricity hovered in the air, making the fine hairs on Órla's arms stand at attention. There had to be a mystical force field around the building. A few feet from the entrance, Roy stopped and fished for something in his pocket. Órla heard a clink of metal, and a flash of light illuminated the air in the shape of a large wall. Another zip of energy sliced through the force field a few feet away, opening a space as wide as a door.

The three of them stepped through the hole, and Órla heard the sizzle of magic as the panel closed behind them. Roy pushed open one side of the heavy oak door and led them into a dimly lit foyer. Sconces cast flickering light across dusty walls and limestone floors. The faint smells of mildew and sweat—like the inside of a locker room—hung in the stale air. In the distance, the murmur of voices echoed through the high ceilings.

Órla's breathing became shallow as the sensation of being trapped overwhelmed her. She stubbornly reigned in her fear and addressed the larger man. "What do you want from me?"

As Roy opened his mouth to speak, a screech like microphone feedback rang through the air. Órla gasped as the sound penetrated not merely her ears, but her brain, like a parasite burrowing into the skin. Nausea rolled in her stomach, and acid rose in her throat. Even Roy grimaced and shook his head against the intrusion.

Words emerged from the squealing, distorted and grotesque. "Put her in the tower until the ritual."

Georgie staggered to the wall and vomited. Órla took deep breaths and willed the nausea to pass, and wondered how a Scotsman with a weak stomach and a kind streak had become a morph kidnapper. The redhead wiped his mouth, cleared his throat, and muttered to himself. "I hate it when Aoife does that."

Aoife. The air demon.

Órla's heart skipped a beat, and her stomach clenched. The legend was true. When King Lir discovered his second wife, Aoife, had turned his children into swans, he became so enraged he banished her as an air demon. Fear sliced through Órla's gut. Why had Aoife returned?

Her knees buckled, and she sagged against the wall. Her vision blurred with tears. Panic gripped her chest in a vice-grip, and the urge to run replaced nausea.

I've been kidnapped by a demon.

Órla tried to pull her wrists out of the handcuffs. Even if she could slip her mystical shackles, outrun Roy and Georgie, and get past the force field . . .

A cruel laugh interrupted her thoughts and echoed through the foyer. More of Aoife's words oozed into her mind, slick and toxic like crude oil. "You can try to run, Órla, but I will drain you like I did the others."

Órla's knees gave out, and she sank down the wall. Blackness swam before her eyes, and the voice faded away. Roy stuck a hand under her armpit and hauled her back to her feet. He shouted in her ear. "Move it."

They wound through a long corridor off the edge of the foyer and climbed a spiral staircase. Every few feet, a rectangular slit in the wall let in some light and cool air from the outside, reminding Órla this wasn't a dream. The air demon had kidnapped her and planned to kill her.

When the muscles in Órla's legs burned, they arrived at the top floor and traveled a hallway lit with sconces until they reached a door of wooden slats. Roy threw it open to reveal a Spartan room, furnished only with a wooden chair and bare bed. Pigeons stirred in the rafters, sending particles of debris floating down from the ceiling, illuminated in shafts of light streaming in through gaps in the shutters.

Her captor roughly pushed her inside and grinned. "Home sweet home."

THE END

NEED ANOTHER MORPHOSIS ME FILE

In the second book of The Morphosis.me Files, A Treacherous Social Game, Kayleigh faces rougher challenges, tougher bullies, and fiercer morphs.

http://samanthamarks.com/novels/

ABOUT THE AUTHOR

Samantha Marks, Psy.D., also known as "Dr. Sam," is a true Renaissance Woman: Clinical Psychologist, Author, Musician, Painter, Mother, Wife.

If you would like to receive an email alert when Dr. Sam's next book is released, sign up at www.samanthamarks.com. Your email address will never be shared, and you can unsubscribe at any time.

Word-of-mouth is crucial for any author to succeed. If you enjoyed this novel, please consider leaving a review at Amazon, or anywhere else online, even if it's only a line or two. Your review will make all the difference and is hugely appreciated.

NOVELS BY SAMANTHA MARKS PSY D

The Morphosis.me Files

A Fatal Family Secret (#1)

A Treacherous Social Game (#2)

A Perilous Blood Allegiance (#3) February 2017

A Noble Clan Legacy (#4) November 2017

SAY HI

Dive further into the world of morphs, see character sketches, and read Kayleigh's blog at www.morphosis.me.

Connect with Dr. Sam at www.samanthamarks.com to get updates, teasers, information on mental health, and other fun things. She can also be found on Facebook, Twitter, LinkedIn, Tumblr, and Instagram.

DR.
SAMANTHA MARKS
PSYCHOLOGY WITH A MAGICAL TWIST

78080910R00159

Made in the USA
Columbia, SC
08 October 2017